This book is the long-awaited second helping of hilarious agricultural ramblings from NFU man, part-time farmer's boy and author of 'Yows and Cows', Mike Sanderson.

The views expressed in this book are the personal views of the author. They in no way relate to NFU policies.

Not S'many Cows and a lot less Yows

Mike Sanderson

HAYLOFT

First published 2004

Hayloft Publishing Ltd, Kirkby Stephen,
Cumbria, CA17 4DJ.

tel: (017683) 42300
fax. (017683) 41568
e-mail: dawn@hayloft.org.uk
web: www.hayloft.org.uk

ISBN 1 904524 08 7

A catalogue record for this book is available
from the British Library

Front cover photograph - Peter Koronka
Back cover photograph - Can-R-Cum

Produced in Great Britain
Printed and bound in Hungary

Acknowledgments

Many of the stories in this book have been previously published in the NFU's 'North West Farmer' or in local newspapers. They are gathered here in a semblance of disorder with cartoons by Paul Gurney, photographs by Can-R-Cum and a drawing of dogs by Kevin Alderson.

Foreword

NOT so many cows and a lot less yows - in the midst of foot and mouth I joked for obvious reasons - this would be the title of my next book. The last thing on my mind at the time was a book but as time has gone on the title is even more poignant as father has now retired and we no longer have Hause Farm or any yows or cows.

What follows is in no real order except that the bits and pieces I wrote in 2001 (foot and mouth year) follow on at the start. It's not really a diary, but reading it you can see how events, and my attitude to them, unfolded.

Mike Sanderson,
December 2003

An early lambing tale

WE were looking for a pet lamb and I called "on spec" on a neighbour's farm at Shap. He wasn't doing the lambing himself but he was good enough to go and have a look in the shed where his son was lambing and fit us up with a fine tup lamb. I took it home, father fitted it up with a skin and new mother, she took to him immediately and within a couple of hours he was mothered on.

The son rang that evening: "Had we got it mothered on?"

"Yes," father said.

"Oh dear," he said, "It's my pedigree tup and I had great hopes for it. But if it's mothered on it wouldn't have to matter."

Father did the decent thing and loaned him the yow for the summer - well we're bound to want another pet lamb sometime.

I must admit this is one of last year's tales but it's taken me this long to pluck up the courage to tell it. Well, father and three sons are big and blonde and they all look down on me.

Squirrel

I think the first thing I wrote in the journal that raised any comment was seeing a fox in the middle of Appleby - similarly one morning recently, staring out of the office window whilst I was on the phone was a red squirrel in the middle of the road dodging about amongst the traffic. I am pleased to say it escaped.

Scanning

WE'RE busy getting ready for lambing and the scanning man made his usual visit. After the horror stories we'd heard about geld yows, father was delighted with the results - 609 scanned, only 26 geld and far too many twins. Can-R-Cum was also pleased with the 150% scan (two yows/three lambs). Both of them are wise enough not to count their chickens. The biggest disappointment was Adrian turning up on time. He'd been out with us at our dinner the night before and I was looking forward to getting after him if he was late.

Going Backwards

Did you see Les Armstrong's guest appearance on *Rural Lives* and more particular his attempts to reverse his quad bike and trailer - still you can't be good at everything!

On the Edge

I'M finishing writing this just as the Foot and Mouth crisis is beginning to look serious. I'm banned from going on farms for obvious reasons and it looks as if it might last for some time yet. It's not going to be easy to keep up with routine work (IACS looming!).

We'll just have to do the best we can. I did suggest to father I might be banned and he told me in no uncertain terms I wasn't banned from Hause Farm and get myself there as there's work to be done. I just hope when I'm reading this, we're getting on top of the job.

Initial thoughts on the Foot and Mouth Crisis

I have been asked to write a piece for this edition on the Foot and Mouth Crisis. As the situation and correct advice changes on an hourly basis, I would like it noting for the records. I am putting this together on Wednesday, 14 March 2001. I hope when we are reading this, I appear to be scare-mongering and everything is "under control" - BUT I doubt it!

At present, we are watching the outbreaks like hawks to see they are not creeping further up the Eden Valley and so far (touch wood) they've not got past Culgaith. The outbreaks around Penrith and Longtown appear to be totally out of control and spreading virtually like wild-fire. It's frightening watching them, but what is more frightening is listening to the tales of the time it takes to get a vet on farm, the time it takes to get the results, the time it takes to get them slaughtered and the days it takes to get them disposed of.

I was speaking to a farmer who had 200+ cattle dead in his buildings and yards just behind the house. They had been dead for four days which would be upsetting enough, but he said he just couldn't start to describe the smell. I know what it's like picking up an old dead yow after a few warm days so that number of cattle doesn't bear thinking about.

From my NFU point of view and having no cases in this area, the main problem has been information, or lack of it. The Ministry of Agriculture can normally send out letters and booklets of no great importance at the drop of a hat, but hardly any information on a subject as important as this has been forthcoming. It took over a fortnight to send out pictures of what foot and mouth looked like and details of exactly what the movement restriction entailed and how these movement licences worked don't seem to have been circulated at all.

The biggest problem with information has been news. There's been truths, half truths, rumour and outright mis-information on possible local outbreaks. I can tell you without exaggeration, at least 50 people have told me Herons at Warcop had foot and mouth. It wasn't rumour or hearsay - it was absolutely definitely a fact. I get details via MAFF and the NFU and had never seen their name, so rang them to check. David assured me it was rubbish. The Ministry had been nowhere near, so goodness knows how the stories start. The Heron boys were quite laid back about it, "if people are talking about us, they weren't talking about anyone else" was the attitude.

Seriously, on this point, if anyone is aware they are being mistakenly talked about, give me a ring as I am often queried and am in a good position to keep folk right.

I am housed in the office as I am not allowed out on to farms for the obvious reasons and I am feeling claustrophobic even with a constant stream of enquiries and visitors to the office. It must be murder on farms hardly daring to leave the farm and only yourself for company. I think they call it stress nowadays.

The most important thing is getting on top of this epidemic, but when the dust settles the big questions are going to be where it came from and how it spread so quickly and easily. I don't think there is any doubt this originated from infected meat from abroad. If rumours again are to be believed, it has got into swill, but with schools and the armed forces allowed to import meat from anywhere, was it not inevitable? There will be a lot of difficult questions to answer by the powers that be.

If anyone was in any doubt what Mr Blair and his cronies think about agriculture, the countryside and rural affairs, the fact they are still seriously considering holding their election amongst all this, puts the tin hat on it. (Is it blatant disregard of us and strutting arrogance?) How can you expect to hold an election in a rural area when folk hardly dare leave their property beggars belief.

Whatever happens, the situation is something akin to kicking a man when he's down - no it isn't - its kicking a man when he's down and then flogging him with a post.

Health Warning

I always like to try and see the funny side of things At present, it's the only thing that keeps me sane. If you have just gone down with foot and mouth, perhaps you shouldn't read on. Don't for one minute think I am taking it lightly - we have lost 150 gimmer hoggs and living and working and farming in this area at present, is like looking down the barrel of a gun.

Communication

IT has been dreadful, but there's been one or two lighter moments. I have been keeping in touch with my members especially our new County Deputy Chairman from Raisgill Hall. He was on the phone and I could hear clicking in the background and told him I thought he was "washing up". He insisted he wasn't and said if he had a video phone he'd show us he was looking for a gate hanging. There was a pause and he decided it wouldn't be a good idea as he did a lot of phoning on the toilet.

We get streams of e-mails and faxes from Veronica at Skelmersdale and all the faxes for reason seem to leave the "V" off the front of her name. I asked her if she'd changed the "N" for a "T" in her name to brighten all our days up. (If you're not sure what I'm on about, try writing it down).

I also keep in regular contact with my colleagues and Martin at Penrith in particular. He was out one particular time so the girls gave me his mobile number which I rang - there was an answer and a little voice came on - "Is that Mike? He's not taken it with him".

Foot Bath

WE have our disinfectant foot-bath at the door which replaces the mat I inherited from Jim, the writing on it faded some time ago, but it did say "All our Visitors make us happy, some by coming, some by going". The foot-bath has found out one or two of my customers with holes in their shoes! They reckon you are most likely to carry the virus in your hair or up your nose, but I haven't plucked up the courage to plunge every visitor's head in a bucket of disinfectant.

Posh house

MY publisher bought a run-down camper from over in the north east. It was so ropey that it was touch and go it would make it to Cumbria. The owner, a young dad, said he'd drive it over but he'd have to get the wife home to watch the baby and his dad, and his dad's mate, to follow him in the car.

The likely lads arrived, with not too much smoke billowing out of the back of the van. Cups of tea and cash were handed over and the young Geordie said: "I knew we were coming somewhere posh with all those carpets on the road!"

On my lead

I am confined to the office apart from my non-farming calls which is driving me demented. Most of my time is spent fielding calls, but I have had a chance to have a bit of a muck out - does anyone want a supply of 1996 calendars? My wife thought it might be good for my figure not partaking in quite as many farmhouse teas. It doesn't seem to be working.

Tax concessions

AS one of the concessions in the crisis, it was said the tax man might be a little forgiving - someone suggested they might mean a second class stamp on the demand.

Happy holidays

I was insuring a caravan for Kevin Buckle who was busy planning his holidays in the midst of the foot and mouth Crisis - lambing sheep at Middlesbrough. His mother spent two months living in the caravan and lambed all the sheep. She wasn't allowed home because of the foot and mouth.

No movements

THE biggest problem out of the actual killing fields has been livestock movements, or lack of them. There are dairy farmers full of wintering sheep. Being a hill man, I don't always feel as sorry for them as I should and told one man the sheep would be OK - they'd have their teeth with them. He did see the funny side - just.

Fat lambs are also a problem. One man was getting upset about the hoteliers complaining. He said: "At least if they've got no guests, they don't have to feed them. I am full of guests I want rid of and I've got to feed them."

Try and look on the bright side - not easy!
I was discussing with Mr Ashley on his garage forecourt the chances of his lambs being culled when "Jones, the Box's" hearse pulled up for petrol. We decided as long as we weren't loaded in the back of that we weren't too bad.

Clean Crows
A lot of people have been blaming crows for spreading the virus, but no one can blame Hause Farm crows as they're the cleanest in the country. All their nests are lined with straw off father's disinfectant mat.

A.I. Bucket
I have been approached by one or two dairy farmers who have no bull and the A.I. man can't come - they're going to lose months on their cows - what could I suggest? The only thing I could come up with was an upturned bucket.

Fingers Crossed
WE will lose 150 gimmer hoggs when Mr Blair finally gets around to murdering them. They're in a 3km zone down at Cliburn, but we should be lambing when you read this - I just hope to hell we've some sheep to lamb.

Still Standing
AS I write these notes on 19 April 2001 we're still standing at Hause Farm - flat out lambing but wondering if we're wasting our time. Even Cam-R-Cum after admiring the newest arrival to her little flock wondered if they'd go into a hole like everyone else's.

A Scare
WE'VE not been without problems. We had a calf feeling very sorry for itself one morning and on close inspection, its mouth was red raw. We convinced ourselves we could see rawness on its feet and feared the worst. We got the MAFF vet out and fortunately it was a false alarm.

The only thing that bothered the vet was I took a shepherding crook and told him it wasn't to catch the calf with but to keep its mother off him. All the time he was inspecting the calf she was circling us with intent.

Lambing

IT'S been hard to concentrate on the lambing with foot and mouth. I've not been able to have my annual holiday. We have been fortunate enough to employ the skills of Bob Mason for the period, better known in local circles as "Bob the Builder". He's doubling up as a child-minder as my two kids are helping in their Easter holidays. I have had it reported to me four MAFF officials in white suits were in our fields. There may well have been two men and two kids in tatty old green coats and a dog trying to run down a cheviot yow - but that's the rumour mill for you!

Bob's lambing

BOB is expecting an addition to his own family in May but has warned his good lady when he is in "lambing mode" he better hadn't find her tilting and paining on the mat when he comes in or things might get on quicker than expected.

Red letter day

OUR last two lambing times have been atrocious and that's being polite. On 11 April we had our best morning for three years. We landed back with the bike and trailer without any carnage. There could be a yow with a hung lamb, a shearling that won't own up to having produced its off-spring, a lamb that refuses to suck, etc,. etc. - take your pick. The only thing we could find to catch was a geld yow trying to pinch a lamb. We were soon back to normal, I hasten to add.

Experts

I think I listened to more than enough boffins and experts on foot and mouth. They all seem to tell a different tale and you begin to wonder which, if any, you should believe. I was given the definition of an expert - EX as in 'has been' and SPURT as 'in drip under pressure'. So now you know all about MAFF 'Exspurts".

Daft?

THERE has been all sorts of reports of farmers and their attitude to their stock but this sums it up for me - the farmer's wife buying bags of milk powder for pet lambs she knows are going on the 3km cull.

Fingers Crossed

I'VE tried to look on the lighter side, but these really have been the worst months of my life. I never thought I'd have to live through anything like this - it's like a bad dream but I can't seem to wake up. Here's fingers crossed there's something left at the end of it all.

Back to Reality

I wrote last month bragging about one morning only finding a geld yow to catch who was pinching lambs - well I have to admit that wasn't the norm. More like normal was one morning towards the end of lambing time, when we had five happy events, one old yow had a pair of twins, that was grand. Two others had twins, one live one and one of the other sort and two shearlings had lambed and bu.... sorry jiggered off. On reflection our lambing was like a lot of others, we were desperate for spring to come and it didn't.

Hay time!

I think our lambing time was summed up on 3 May. Our old girls usually loose interest in hay in the middle of April but I went to fill a hay rack where the last seventy or so yows were lambing and three quarters of them came like silly beggars. That's for hay not feed.

Frustration

EVERYONE who has had to deal with MAFF in the last three to four months has my sympathy. My favourite tale was ringing the State Veterinary Service for some advice. It rang for ages and then I was advised the call was being diverted. I eventually got a foreign sounding gentlemen and when I explained my problem he advised me I needed a different number and he gave me it.

Now I have a list of all the contact numbers in front of me so could tell him the number he had given me was the MAFF fax number. He gave me another number and I politely explained that was for movement licences. He gave me another number and that was also for licences. Ahh - he'd now got the right number - I had to very politely explain that was his number, the number I'd just rung so there was little point in continuing the conversation. I ask you?

Names

WE'VE had Phoenix the calf, Porky the pig and goodness knows what else. So when speaking to our MP's wife we asked if her husband could ask the Minister if my father gave all his 650 sheep names would they be exempt from any cull? With us being busy lambing, we've been calling them all sorts of names, but probably not names that would impress Tony.

Compensation

I keep getting asked if MAFF are going to compensate for cattle going over 30 months, extra keep on wintering sheep and the like and I can assure you the NFU are working on it. My wife reliably informs me my bald patch is twice as big as it was at Christmas and what hair I have left is twice as grey. Am I going to be compensated - that's what I want to know.

Stood to Attention

I'VE kept in constant touch with my colleagues at Carlisle as I have found being at the centre of operations, they're the best source of information. My mate, Wendy Harrison, has been going into the Army Ops room to be de-briefed (I think that's what they call it) and can then confirm or quash the rumour mills for me. I don't like to bother Mr Utting as he's obviously very busy but was allowed to talk to him on an odd occasion if I stood to attention and didn't wind him up - I managed the standing to attention bit.

A sore thumb

It's been cold lambing and I managed to get a keen/kin in the end of my left thumb. Quite an achievement for a pen pusher! I thought it was quite painful as it was my pen-pushing hand until I got the thumb on my right hand between a Cheviot yow in full flight and the mesh gate in the back of the bike trailer. It tore all the skin off the side of my thumb and at present, the nail can't decide if it wants to come off or not.

T for triplet

WE don't get many sets of triplets and those we do get are usually a waste of time. We did get a reasonable set and we usually number or letter twins so these were put out with T's on them - for triplet. I thought that was handy and could soon be used for 'T' for twins and if things got worse 'T' for "t'only one left". If I remember correctly, she ended up with twins an one got mothered onto another yow.

MAFF men

HOW many MAFF men does it take to change a light bulb?

Two - one to assure you everything is under control and one to screw the light bulb into the tap!

On the wane???

AS I write this on 18 May things do seem to be dying down but life gets no easier on the fringes with livestock movements and silaging etc. becoming real problems. I have heard it many times and am sure it's true. "It's those that haven't got it who've got all the headaches". I only hope it doesn't mysteriously burst out again on 8 June.

Yows and Cows

PEOPLE keep asking me if I'm writing another book. I've not done much about it, but I've got a title "Not so many cows and a lot less yows".

By a thread

WE hoped it wouldn't happen, but as I write foot and mouth is ripping through our area like wild fire. We are the country's hot spot. We've been watching it for four months and now the tension is almost unbearable, you shouldn't have to live like this. At Hause Farm we're like an island on Crosby Ravensworth Common, contiguous to nothing bar the fell so I guess we stand or fall, live or die with the common. With disease all around we're hanging on by a thread. Fingers crossed/touch wood.

Run in!

WHAT follows was written a couple of weeks ago so please take it in the spirit it was intended.

Father was most upset when he got a call from the ministry telling him they wanted to inspect his sheep as they'd been reported as being ill on the fell. He assured them they were OK but they came and inspected them anyway - looking in their mouths and at their feet, talking temperatures and the like but they couldn't find anything wrong.

Father couldn't find out who'd run him in but after much badgering they did admit it was a visitor and they of course have an extensive knowledge of animal health matters! When we thought about it there had been an old geld yow kicking about on the roadside who had started to thrive and cast a bit of wool and to the untrained eye might look a bit dodgy. At one stage she was making a passable impression of Lenny the Lion.

The ex-County Chairman
WRITING these pieces is much harder this year. Last year when I was stuck for inspiration I just poked fun at my mate Harold from Wigton. I am pleased to say, as of now, he's still one of the few out that way who've kept clear of foot and mouth but I understand he's got other things to think about - like untangling his rowing-up machine out of the dyke!! Best of luck Harold.

Maestro
MY wife is the proud owner of an E-reg Maestro which cost the princely sum of £700 over five years ago, that's what I call motoring. My garage man was inspecting it with a view of MOT-ing it again and told me it was the worst damned car he'd ever sold - it was supposed to drop to bits after two years.

DEFRA
I know none of us thought much about MAFF but this new organisation frightens the life out of me. With all its responsibilities it looks as if farming could just be a little fish in a big pond. I hope it is DEFRA and not DAFTER. I have been told if you pronounce DEFRA correctly is should sound like "death row". I've been racking my brains as to what it really stands for and the best I can come up with is Destroy Every Farm Round About. I'm sure there's better.

Did you hear what happened to the Royal family in Nepal? - MAFF got the wrong grid reference.

Bare pasture

ONE of my more thinking members likened British farming to a horse that's a bad catch. What do you do with a horse that's too headstrong and you can't make much of it - put it on a bare pasture then it's grateful for any morsel and it's good to catch. I think we're on the bare pasture lads!!

Fancy a pig?

I was relieved to hear from an expert they haven't been able to pass foot and mouth from an animal to a person, to a second person and then on to an animal. They didn't quite describe it to us like this, but it's the picture I had in my mind's eye: Vet no. 1 snogs pig with foot and mouth, vet no. 1 snogs vet no. 2, vet no. 2 does his best to pass it on but so far they haven't managed. You would find it easier to pass it on in muck so for goodness sake make sure you're clean if you do venture out.

Toe

I was complaining last month about losing the nail on my thumb, well I've done a bit better than that since. I was dragging the manure drill into a corner to tidy things up. I gave one yank and it only moved a foot, so I gave a bigger one and it came two foot and landed on my big toe. My boots offered no protection so I ended up with a swollen toe, a purple nail and a marked limp. Not fit out I think I was told.

Therapy

WE have not had much hay or clipping weather. We don't know if we should be among our sheep or not so I've been looking for a job of a weekend. I ended up doing something I haven't done for a while, mowing thistles by hand.

I took my son with me and just told him to practise his cricket strokes. If he was short of motivation just think of the French master or the headmaster. It's good therapy for farmers too - Tony Blair, Nick Brown, Margaret Beckett - chop, down they all went. Young James soon got the hang of it: "Dad why when you've cut one do you turn round and ten more have grown?"

A frayed thread

LAST month I wrote about hanging on by a thread, well it's a bit frayed now but it is still holding out, just. The common seems to be surrounded with disease so crunch time will come when we test the fell!

Under scrutiny

AS the disease has got nearer at home we have been increasingly pestered with vets, but we have done our best to comply even though their organisational skills don't fill you with confidence. We agreed to have our sheep blood tested and half way through bleeding 180 yows another surveillance vet landed, a Spaniard I think. Now father is a tremendous good hand at chasing unwanted reps and the like, but struggled with this young man. In the end he had to get the vet who was bleeding the sheep and father said something along the lines: "I can mek nowt o' that so and so, you'd better see to him," even the Ministry vet struggled with him.

The weekend after we had a little Canadian girl to look at our stock. We caught sheep, looked cows, answered questions, coloured maps and I even scrubbed her back. She hadn't been gone half an hour and we were having our coffees when the phone went - another vet wanting to come and look - I ask you.

There's a couple of apt sayings. One about the left hand not know what the right hand is doing and another about drunken parties in breweries.

Rumours

THERE have been many tales doing the rounds but I like the one best of the lady vet who strips down to her underwear to disinfect. I haven't seen it myself but do know the County Vice Chairman has put in a complaint as he doesn't see why he should have a sixty-year-old male vet.

Dirty video

FATHER got his video from the ministry. He looked at it very carefully, shook it, rattled it and held it up to the light, but couldn't make anything of it. Video recorders haven't reached Hause Farm yet. As one or two have said they'd have been better sending a gallon of disinfectant instead.

Arise Sir Nick

WE are all aware of what a marvellous job Nick has done at Carlisle through this whole foot and mouth carry on and I am sure we would be in a bigger pickle in Cumbria without him. Someone was telling me he could see him becoming Lord Utting of Watermillock after this is over, at least I think that's what he said - or it could have been 'Nick Utting, what a pillock'.

The cure

DEFRA in their wisdom have come up with the cure for foot and mouth and they've named it after where they discovered it. It's called the "Crosby Ravensworth Cure" and it's worked. It guaranteed no-one in Crosby will go down now and they almost worked the magic in Shap and by the time you read this, it could well have worked up Stainmore and around Drybeck (to those who don't know the area, Crosby has been totally cleaned out and in my perverted way of looking at it the "Crosby Ravensworth Cure" is to kill absolutely everything). See picture page 59.

Still Hanging On

WE'VE lost a few yows to a dangerous contact but the rest are still there on the common and on our inside ground in the middle of the common. The ministry seem confident there's no disease there but I have my doubts. There's only four commoners out of twenty NOT got it. They've had six culls of the fell and two have shown foot and mouth and the bigger half of the boundary has had disease up to it! When you're reading this we will know as we are about to blood test. I hope to report they were right and I was wrong.

Poor Pugwash

FOUR years ago we had a cheviot lamb born with a perfect black circular patch around it's eye. It was quite unusual and the kids christened it "Pugwash" after Captain Pugwash the cartoon pirate who had an eye patch. It turned out to be a gimmer and got kept even though it was not as big as the others just because we all know it and Can-R-Cum took a shine to it. She had a habit of getting kessen when she was coming up to lamb so rather than turn her back to the fell after they were scanned, this time she got up on our allotment so father could keep an eye on her.

That allotment is the only bit we've lost so far to foot and mouth so doing our best for poor Pugwash didn't work out too well. Her only consolation was, if she didn't have that patch on her eye, she'd have gone as a fat lamb four years ago.

A dirty farmer
THEY cleared the allotment I have been talking about above and true to form missed a lamb. Father informed them and they asked him if he knew a dirty farmer who would get it in for them. This tickled him and he said he knew a few but they'd all have to have at least two baths a year.

Eric the Blue
I think the only good thing to report on the farming front is we got our hay very nicely despite a breakdown or two. You get this ancient tackle out after 51 weeks and expect it to go like mad for a week and it doesn't' always. What was unusual was the weather didn't catch us out when we did have a breakdown.

We had an addition to our bale leading staff this year. You've heard of "Eric the Red" the famous Viking, this is "Eric the Blue", the famous Carlisle United supporter. Anyone who knows Eric knows he talks like a machine gun. I assure you he throws bales like one as well. The crack was good and they made short work of them.

A new language
IF you'd have said this to the wife last year, she'd have thought you'd taken leave of your senses: "I know my bio-security isn't up to much, but if I get into the bathroom and thoroughly detox myself, can we get contiguous?" Just shows how things have changed.

Number 2000
YOU probably read my comments last month regarding the ministry's confidence that our fell was clean of foot and mouth. It gives me no great pleasure to report that I was right and they were wrong. As you may have seen, we had the distinction of being the 2000th case and got all the publicity that went with it - I don't suppose it did any harm, but I could have done without it. I have talked to lots of folk who have gone down and hundreds who have lost their stock, but I can tell you something, nothing prepares you for when it happens to you.

The hardest part

WITHOUT doubt, the hardest part of the whole carry on was to take my daughter the night before the cull to take some photos on digital of her old black yow and lamb and then to have to look at them penned up the next day, it certainly wasn't easy. We've got (touch wood) 270 yows and lambs left on our inside land so it's just about bearable.

Thanks

I would just like to thank everyone for all their kindness through this, both to myself, Dad and Mam. At home we have had dozens of phone calls, messages and the like offering support and it is much appreciated.

Just to finish the whole sad escapade off, I have fallen heir to a very nice horn handled shepherd's stick that was left on the day of the cull at the Orton end of the top of the "Ruck" - if you know whose it is let me know.

Get away byeeee.....

POOR old Rap is now aged fourteen or more and his selective deafness has just about turned into permanent deafness. He still likes to go with you and work and as long as you're doing things the way you usually do them, he's still more than useful. The problem is when you're not doing things as usual and you've got both dogs out. Glen tends to follow the old dog and even if he's wrong and you're yelling at him, he thinks Rap's right and you're wrong. After a busy holiday weekend among the sheep, I was hardly able to speak after shouting for three days solid.

Dog running qualifications

ON a similar subject, I took son James with me to Cockermouth to watch Penrith play rugby. The home supporters were venting their fury at the referee who had one of their players sent off and three sin-binned. The language was choice and James thought they might be good at running a dog.

Stupid peasants

WE'VE now had nine months of foot and mouth and I have listened to countless experts, vets and scientists, read dozens of articles and papers on the subject and there's only one thing I can tell you for sure. The more I find out the less I understand.

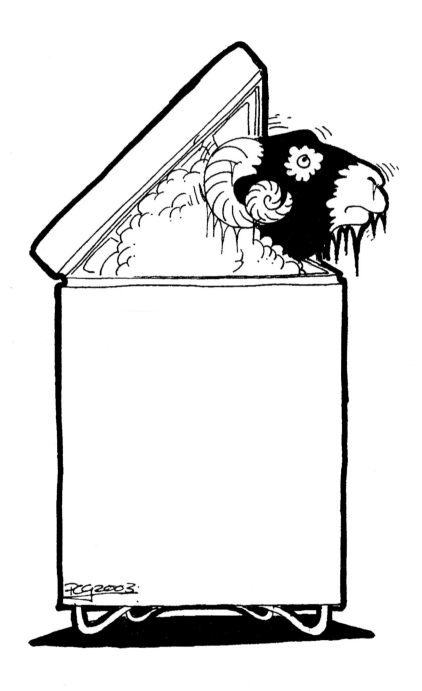

I sometimes think they think us peasants are stupid. They tell us something one week and tell us something different a month later and expect us not to remember what we were told in the first place!

A breed for the future

EVERY farm that goes down with foot and mouth is a disaster, but the one that's caused most grief locally is George and David Dent with their Dairy Shorthorns at Winton. I think I have had the most comment especially from the non-farming community and now realise that there was a lot more than me used to ride past and enjoy looking at them. We can only hope their heifers up Mallerstang survive and it's not too long before we can see them again.

It tickled me when David put a cow on show for us when we had our farming display in the auction at Kirkby Stephen. He put up a board listed all the Shorthorns attributes and titled it "A Breed for the Future" - I hope so.

Chilled ram

I was asked if I thought it would be OK to move a chest freezer in a cattle trailer. I thought carefully, not under 'A' Notice, Vehicle and Trailer detoxed. Yes OK - as long as there wasn't a TUP in it. (I did find out later, there WAS a tup in it.)

Happy Birthday

I am writing these notes on my birthday. It's depressing enough at my age and it doesn't help when you get cards like Tina's which suggested I have got to the stage where I grow more hair out of my nose than out of the top of my head. Can-R-Cum's was no better and went something like "Happy Birthday Dad, I think you're cool," then open it up - "It's everyone else who thinks you're a Prat." Wonderful!

Back to square one

I reported last month we were down to 270 yows. We've still half a dozen cows and poor old father was reflecting on the situation and decided it maybe wasn't too bad. It was about what he'd set off with at Hause Farm in 1956.

Bring a broiler

I went to and was very impressed with Carlisle NFU's do in the chicken shed. Nick's "Bring a Broiler Night" I think it should have been called. Twelve hundred people under one roof, all fed and watered, the organisation was superb. I suggested if DEFRA had organised it we would all have had a packet of crisps in the car park. Someone else thought his crisps would probably be a fortnight in coming. There was quite a queue of farmers to get in. Someone thought it might be a DEFRA plot, get us all in, shut the doors and turn on the gas!!

Heaping slurry

ONE disgruntled farmer was telling me he was struggling to get a slurry licence and our friends at Carlisle suggested he heaped it up. I thought it would be a good job for all of them down there - half with a bucket and half with a shovel - heaping slurry.

Yows and cows and boffins

WHAT about that carry on over cattle and sheep brains? For anyone interested a yow brain (yes, she has one) is rather bigger than a tennis ball. A cow brain is rather less than a football and the researcher's is something akin to a small pea. Our lives are in their hands!

All the best - you deserve it

WELL, we are getting to the end of 2001, thank goodness. We have been to hell and back and none of us have seen a year like it or want to see another. It's been like walking into the unknown blindfolded and I guess next year could be something similar.

A funny horse

DID you hear about the local farmer pulled up by a DEFRA patrol for leaving cow muck on the road? He completed a very heated argument by explaining it was the first time he'd ever seen cow muck come out of a horse's bottom. I'm not sure that's quite how he phrased it though.

EC directive 2002

I hope you realise after New Year this new directive will come into being and you will no longer be able to spend a penny - you will have to "euro-nate".

Devastation

I have done a very rough FMD survey of the farms in this branch and I reckon:

- 60% have lost everything or almost everything
- 20% have all or the majority of their stock left
- 20% are somewhere in between.

Lucky lambs

QUITE a few of our 270 yows that escaped DEFRA had twin lambs so we've managed to scratch 150 gimmer hoggs together as normal. We normally pick 150 from 300 or so, but this year we only had 170 to pick from so as you can imagine there are some lucky little lambs that wouldn't normally have been kept. On the whole they're not at all bad. I am sure the tups don't think they're quite as lucky with nine of them for 270 yows. There'll be questions asked if there's too many geld yows.

Unbelievable

SOME questions asked by DEFRA before issuing a licence:

- You've missed filling part of the form, what sex is your bull?
- We need to know if your tups have aborted before they can be moved.
- You can only move your wool if it hasn't been in contact with any sheep.

And my favourite:

Q. Will your bull come into contact with any other animals once it has been moved?
A. I sincerely hope so!

And a local joke: What's the difference between a dead dog and a dead DEFRA man lying in the road - there's skid marks by the dog.

There was a joke doing the rounds that DEFRA staff had been fit up with a Britains catalogue so they would know what a telescopic handler or an excavator was. It wouldn't be a bad idea and might just avoid statements like: "Yes, you can have a licence to move your sheep but who are Ifor Williams and David Brown?"

Light my pyre

I can vouch for the above, but I'm not sure if these two are right but they make good reading.

A man is hired early on by the ministry and his first job is to source sleepers for pyres. It's not easy as there's great demand but he finds some in Kent. They cost a bit to transport up to Cumbria but that's OK. They came to unload them in Cumbria and there's only one problem - they're CONCRETE.

They are having problems finding sleepers for pyres so would use wooden doors and then couldn't work out why they didn't burn too well - they were FIRE RESISTANT doors.

Clean up job

ONE farmer was complaining bitterly he had eventually got permission to move his tup and his licence ran for 27 pages. He went on to complain how much sawdust he had to use to satisfy his Field Office that no "liquid" would run out of his trailer. I suggested that was perhaps what the 27 pieces of paper were for.

The battle of the Penrith spur, 2001, a personal view from up the valley, written for the Cumberland & Westmorland Herald, Christmas 2001

THE title sounds a bit like a history lesson and let's hope it is. In the Upper Eden Valley, the early fight against foot and mouth was a spectator sport. We watched it blaze away around Carlisle, Penrith and Wigton, by Easter the line came up the valley as far as Appleby and Kings Meaburn and then came to a halt. There were the outbreaks around Musgrave and Brough with the devastating repercussions locally, but it looked as if most of the area might escape the plague.

We, all then know what happened next. It sneaked in round by Meaburn and Crosby Ravensworth and the whole of our area was on fire. Our friends at DEFRA who I'll come to later christened our area the "Penrith Spur" and the whole of the Upper Eden Valley was laid waste too. There have been odd pockets left but the vast majority of the farms and the livestock went down. We've probably been the hardest hit of anywhere.

Did you hear the one...

DID you hear the one about the Englishman, the Irishman and the Scotsman, the Spaniard and the South African, the Canadian, the Aussie and the Kiwi? Well, they are all vets and they've all been to Hause Farm. I have dealt with a lot of them myself, just the sight of them makes father angry, so we have tried to book them in over the weekends. In general, the vets on the ground have been brilliant. We have had no cause to fall out or get angry with them, but what back up have they had.

Every time they come with their paperwork and every time they ask the same questions, whether they'd know if you told them something different every time I don't know, probably not. We agreed early on to allow them to do a surveillance blood test and were half way through bleeding the sheep, when another vet turned up demanding to do a surveillance visit. Father couldn't chase him and he's a good hand at that and the vet who was doing the bleeding struggled to get rid of him.

I know how many "cock ups" we had at Hause Farm in our little corner of the world. I also know we were no different to anyone else so when you multiply it up over the county it doesn't bear thinking about.

There are many conspiracy theories, (Mr bin Laden started it and Mr bin Laden finished it!) but I don't go with that. I just put it down to total incompetence. We all felt it had about burnt itself out when it did stop, it was up a lot of dead ends with no stock left to run in. It added insult to injury when the ministry tried to put it down to their increased biosecurity and not the obvious. MAFF were supposed to be acquiring wood sleepers before the outbreak and were supposed to be drawing up a contingency plan - All I can think is, if they had a plan it was a damned poor one.

If anyone thinks they'll find any consistency or logic in anything that's gone on they'll be sadly disappointed. I thought I'd got my head around foot and mouth after about a month but the more I was told the less I understood - no two experts seem to have the same opinion!

A plan

I know from dealing with MAFF or DEFRA in my position with the NFU about their forward planning. We have tried to forewarn them of problems that were going to arise, but rather than be prepared, they only seemed to think about it a fortnight after something should have been done.

Be it licences to move stock, gathering the commons or to bring sheep back for clipping, dipping or welfare, they were always running behind time. Tup licences were the worst example. It didn't take a genius to work out come October, farmers would need to buy and move tups. In July, we explained sensibly, we pleaded, we banged the table, we got cross. Nothing happened. We explained a licensing system was better than them moving in the night because at least they would know where they were. I even tried humour. If they couldn't supply a licence, can we have baseball caps and sunglasses so the tups can sit in the front of a Land Rover or pick-up undetected.

As everyone knows who tried to move tups, what we got was far too little too late, but for goodness sake don't blame us lads for not trying.

Changing moods

I think, in hindsight, the strangest thing about the whole fiasco is how well the whole farming community accepted the situation. I suppose everyone was virtually imprisoned on their own farm, and although folk kept in touch, it's not the same as half a dozen folk getting together. I think people were shell-shocked and certainly I know from experience and talking to others, that if you went down and the system clicked into gear, you were just sidelined - all the vets, field officers, slaughter men, tackle etc., etc., overwhelmed you.

As the year has worn on, the attitude has got more agitated and farmers have got more cheesed off. You could understand when the whole system to deal with foot and mouth was thrown together there would be problems, but you would hope after six months, it would run a bit more smoothly. It didn't. If anything, it was worse.

Our friends in Government were running a P.R. campaign against the farmer which didn't help. Spin, I think they call it. For a while, every week brought another spate of false accusations, valuations, farmers spreading disease, cleaning up costs etc. They had to back track on them all eventually, but in some cases, the damage was done.

Restocking

INITIALLY, a lot of farmers weren't going to rush back in and restock. They'd wait there for four months or even more and certainly weren't going to be bothered with sentinels. Well, farmers being farmers, seeing all that grass going to waste, looking at empty fields far too long made

them badly so most have got back as soon as they could. Whether it's the
right thing to do or not or what is the right thing to do will take a wiser
man than me to tell you.

I've been to a few of these regeneration meetings and all I can tell you
is I'm sure the rest of them are no wiser than me, but they want to stick
their oar in. The environmentalist, the bird men, the walkers and the rest
all see this as their opportunity to have the countryside THEY presum-
ably want. They'll be to watch.

TV
With working for the NFU, appearing on TV is one of the hazards of the
job which I can usually manage without too much fuss. The interview on
the day our fell sheep were culled wasn't easy, but every time Border
News talk about foot and mouth you see our fell sheep being gathered for
the cull.

Just a start
I know I've only scratched the surface and you could write pages about
the politics, the rights and wrongs of culls and vaccination and much,
much more, but I've written far more than I have been asked to now.

Who's the boss?
I often write about our dog Rap and usually crack him up but he does
have his moments! A perfect example was recently when we were gathering sheep on an allotment into the pens. We've done it dozens of times
before and he knows the job off by heart and you needn't really run him.
This particular day I'm sure he'd decided to test the old man's patience.
If father stopped him he carried on, if he sent him left he went right. At
one stage he was stood in among the yows with his head on one side
looking at father as if he didn't have a clue what he was doing.

It wasn't as if they were yows with young lambs that take a bit of handling or newly spained lambs that can make a fool of the best of dogs,
just a few old yows that were supposed to be getting fat.

Father shouted 'till he couldn't shout anymore. He would probably
have done better keeping quiet and letting him do his own thing. He got
crosser and crosser and me and Can-R-Cum couldn't help but laugh so
he got even crosser. I'm not just sure what he was up to that day, but he
got his ears boxed for his troubles and the next time we gathered that

allotment he ran to perfection.

The field in question is on the roadside and just what any holiday-makers would have made of it if they'd stopped for a picnic goodness only knows. If they'd a camcorder there would certainly have been enough material to earn a shilling or two on *You've Been Framed.* They might have learned a word or two they hadn't heard before or possibly thought they'd come across an escaped inmate from a mental hospital. Come the middle of April it could well be the case if the lambing weather is anything like the last two years!

Me book
AS you can hardly have failed to have noticed I've had a book out, you could hardly have missed the publicity and I've been extremely pleased with the way the local press and media have picked up on it - even a spot on Border News and Lookaround.

There's been amusing moments along the way; filming the dog running was a good one. I'd normally set him off, if he hadn't already set off himself and then follow him up the field and give him a hand out with the sheep. The cameraman wanted me to stand still while he filmed but I'd started walking without thinking and it took four takes before they were happy.

The field was really wet and the handiest sheep were a batch of store lambs, one or two of them were a bit slow so it wasn't the best of jobs. By the time we were finished Rap was a bit sick and I'm sure from the way he looked at me he was thinking: "Do you want these damned lambs fetching or not?" I had to give them a bit of a warning to make sure the dog looked at his best as he has a reputation to keep up.

My mate Mr Pigney told me he kept his copy by his bed. This quite surprised me as I could see it would have powers of amusement if you were given to agricultural humour, but I couldn't see how it could help with marital matters. He put me right though - he would read a page or two when he couldn't sleep! One of the only complaints was from the scanning man who claimed it had a detrimental effect on his marital matters, his wife would go to bed and curl up with my book and ignore him.

The press reports have all been very encouraging but I must admit I don't think they'd be as kind if I wrote for a living. *The Messenger* report took the biscuit. The girls were good enough to give me a write up but a mis-print had me losing my son's hamper in the back of the gas fire and not his HAMSTER.

Father was visited by his landlord just into the New Year - the Earl of Lonsdale - and even he had got a copy for Christmas. I'm not sure whether this is a claim to fame or not.

I've had plenty of feedback, a lot wanting to know when I'm retiring on the proceeds, but I can assure you I'd have to write more than this in a year to earn a living and keep a wife and two teenagers. I've also received a nice letter or two, one from my predecessor's predecessor. I'm sure one or two of my older clients will remember Alan Birkbeck. I've also received a nice letter from a farmer in Lancashire along with a cartoon from his grandson - The Sheep's Revenge.

Even father has got into the act, a time or two he's been approached by folk he doesn't really know - something along the lines of "You're a gay old bugger you. I've just been reading about you." He's getting quite proud of the fact he's known as the man who only has three baths a year.

Xmas

THE timing was just right for Christmas and what do you buy a smelly old farmer for his Christmas Box!! There's not that much choice. I was told I was being put in people's stockings, now I ask you, what would I look like in stockings!

We've had a pretty quiet Christmas with son James getting a bike and Can-R-Cum a digital camera and she reckons she's busy taking pictures for the next book. The most appreciated gift this year has been the fish tank for Can-R-Cum's goldfish that has survived since Appleby Show Day!!

It's progressed from a mixing bowl to it's new tank much to the delight of the cat which sits the day by the length watching. It's that keen we've christened the tank CAT TV.

Computer wizardry

WHEN I do one of these articles on the computer I run the computer spell-checker over it to correct all my mistakes. To the uninitiated the machine has a dictionary in its brain and it goes through the piece and picks out any of the spellings it doesn't recognise and gives you alternative correct spellings. A lot of the local words I use it doesn't like and also a lot of place names and people's names. For example in this piece it wanted to change Mr Pigney to Mr Pygmy - which all goes to show how much computers know, he's some pygmy!!

Mowdies

MOLES aren't the sort of thing you would normally get excited enough to write about but a recent experience has changed that. I think my first memory of dealing with moles is not the animal itself but worms. Father used to poison them for my grandfather and I can remember following the plough on Shap gathering jars of worms so he could add strychnine to them and put paid to their unsightly mess.

You might wonder what we were doing with a plough on Shap but all sorts of rocky fields seemed to get put down to rape and kale when I was a kid. For anyone who's not sure why moles are a pest if they're allowed to run wild you can end up with more mole heaps than grass in your field and sheep and cattle aren't too keen on eating soil. Mole heaps can also do damage to hay time and silaging equipment and soil in silage can poison sheep.

Other early memories take me back to when I started tractor driving in my early teens and everything in sight got chain-harrowed. I had a harrowing experience when I levelled a field of mole heaps only to discover it had a number of traps in it which were now bent and scattered all over the field.

I also remember James my son when he was young in the hay field picking up a dead mole which must have been tapped by the hay bob as it was unmarked. He thought it was lovely and soft and was going to keep him but reality soon cut in. Moley wasn't quite as an attractive proposition next day when he started to stink. He was soon consigned to the dustbin.

The alterative to poisoning them is catching and trapping them, and farmers or the men hired in to catch them, often like to show the pride they take in their job and the fact they have taken the time to do it by hanging them on a roadside fence. I guess the reason might also be if you've been hired in to catch them that you've actually done your job. Another alternative is shooting them but I've only ever seen it done once and I'm sure it was down to pure luck, father didn't reckon so though.

There's a nice story of Ken Carruthers, a local haulier who is extremely proud of his garden and a couple of agricultural jokers who sneaked in overnight with buckets of topsoil and created a molehill or two. There was a temper tantrum or two and some serious investigations before he got to the bottom of it.

The reason I've been driven to go on about moles is under a string of them on my father's allotment fence wound into the ideal wire just a week or two ago was a bunch of flowers. Not some old cast offs but a spray of newly purchased roses from a florists still wrapped in the fancy cellophane and paper. Now you sometimes see tributes like this left when there's been a car accident and someone has been killed but nothing like that had happened on this piece of road so we can only presume they were left for the poor moleys. Mind I don't suppose it would be poor little moley if he was throwing up heaps in their garden!

No wonder we have trouble with the anti-hunters when people can take this attitude over moles. Walt Disney and Rolf Harris have a lot to answer for.

Hunting for a Reason

ON being asked to write a piece on hunting and giving the matter a little thought it strikes me the difference between the varying viewpoints all come down quite simply to knowledge. When I say knowledge, I mean practical working experience of countryside matters, not just hunting. The true countryman, which is certainly not the same thing as someone who lives in the country in a sanitised bungalow or in a dormitory village, lives and works hand in glove with nature.

The farmer, gamekeeper, shepherd etc. see nature for what it truly is.

It is not at all kind and certainly not what the general public perceive as nature. It is quite simply the survival of the fittest and the devil take the hindmost. Just look at the bad publicity the pussy cat has had recently for killing everything it comes across, still pussy needn't worry, he's pretty and fluffy and doesn't wear a red jacket or look life a toff. When you witness nature at first hand on a regular basis you come across hunting situations all the time and killing a fox is no better or worse than many others. I wouldn't say it's pretty or a peaceful way to go about it but it's a lot better than an awful lot of other deaths and a lot better than many of the alternatives if hunting was to go.

A fox is vermin and does I can assure you take lambs and create havoc in chicken runs - just for fun. They do have to be kept down. I can't speak for hunting throughout the whole country but certainly in Cumbrian mountains they don't just hunt for fun. Just weigh up where we'd be if the six Cumbria Fell Packs didn't exterminate a hundred foxes plus apiece a year. Get your calculator out and reckon up where we'd be if after ten years they had all lived and all bred - up to our necks in foxes!

Cumbrian hunt supporters don't follow the widely held view that they're all upper class, retired majors or lorded gentry. They're generally working men and women going about their hobby which their forebears have been doing for generations before them, solving a natural problem in a natural way. Are these folk criminals? Should they be made into criminals, surely not! Traditional ways are disappearing fast enough without any further encouragement.

Rural communities are being overrun by former town and city dwellers escaping and then wanting the countryside they find to be the countryside they want, no nasty smells and noises and certainly not out of hours. I know of more than one village where moves are afoot to have cows on foot banned because they will do what cows do.

It always amazes me that the "antis" can get in such a stew about putting vermin down when there are far more pressing cases of inhumanity, but by mankind to mankind. Why not start and worry about the pretty furry fox after you've sorted out atrocities to humans. That of course is the crux of the matter, if foxy wasn't pretty and furry but looked something akin to a rather large rat I doubt we'd be having this debate.

I'd quite happily argue all of the above points with anyone but the unfortunate thing is reasoned argument whether you agree with it or not is completely irrelevant here. It seems New Labour has moved so far from its traditional roots it's throwing them the hunting community as a few crumbs of comfort. Do the powers that be think more of the fox (and homosexuals) than the countryman, agriculture, pensioners, families, motorists, industry, the health service, education, education, education........ etc.

I believe and hope we'll be counting the marchers in London in many hundreds of thousands, which other cause can move as many?

18th March

EDDIE "Tally Ho" Braithwaite has asked me to remind everyone of the March in March. Transport is being arranged from Appleby and you can get in touch on 017683 51694. As he quite rightly says, if the powers that be get their own way it could be the last "Tally Ho". I, for one, certainly don't want my life ruled by the urban majority who see the countryside and animals through either the eyes of Walt Disney or Rolf Harris. Ignorance is a wonderful thing! If you can go, do. I certainly am.

The things you see when you haven't got a camera

FOR everyone reading this in the North of the County in the Bampton area you'll never guess what I saw between Xmas and the New Year in Kirkby Stephen - Wendy Harrison pushing a pram - and it didn't half suit her. I stopped to ask her what she'd been up to, but she swore blind it was nothing to do with her.

Looking for the form

YOU should have got your Sheep Premium form in by now, but don't panic if you've missed the HLCA form. There wasn't one. They'll work it off the IACS form. Uncle Bryan and Auntie Jean had a full scale fall out when they couldn't find it.

What a way to celebrate

ONE of the more unusual ways seen to celebrate the festive season - big baling silage. I never did find out off Stan if it was first cut 2001 or fourth cut 2000!

Three things

JOHN Taylor from Low Howgill is a stickler for detail and was busy playing war over moving his suckler cows on to another holding. There were three things he had to remember: to advise MAFF, to advise the RCMS at Workington and to get a fancy letting agreement. I had to disagree - there were four things John - no there isn't - yes there is - DON'T forget to load your cows into the trailer and take them.

Magnificent MAFF

I'M writing this tight up to the deadline so things might have moved on but what are MAFF busy doing? Writing to loads of farmers whose farms straddle the LFA line telling them they will have to keep more stock if they want to draw their Hill Sub. This is the fancy new area scheme where the idea is you keep less stock and lose no sub. - brilliant!! I've just spoken to Peter Allen who's sure he can sort it out with the help of staff in London. I hope by now he's right and we can sing his praises.

Auntie Jean

MY Auntie Jean was retiring from Christian Head and I was asked to put a poem together for her leaving do. This was my best attempt:

> From Brough Castle Farm
> I received a request
> It wouldn't be easy
> But I'd do my best
>
> Could I write a poem
> About my Auntie Jean
> Please make it funny
> But keep it clean
>
> Whether it's sheep or folk
> She's a tremendous worker
> With an eye for detail
> And never a shirker
>
> She's worked long and hard
> At Christian Head
> Beyond the call of duty
> It's true to be said

She's worked a few years
Over her quota
She's done her fair share
On the old staff rota

Now the time's come
To celebrate her work
And let her party
As a bit of a perk

The big question is
Will she actually retire
And stay with her sheep
Deep in the mire?

Will she retire?
Or will she wait?
Till she's old enough
To be an inmate

Or will she work so long
She's still on the staff
When someone there's
Got to give her a bath

Would she rather be
At Christian Head
Or beating Uncle Bryan
About the head?

Never mind the future
Just raise your glass
To my Auntie Jean
She's a grand old lass.

Happy New Year

I write this just prior to Christmas and have never seen our farm at Shap as wet. We usually reckon at a thousand feet and on limestone our rain fast becomes someone else's problem, but not this year. At present there's water standing on hillsides and it's a full time job washing the dog who has now moved into the house following a recent illness.

New fangled

I was amused by my agricultural engineer friend across the town who had sold a bike with a cab. The cab was in a flat-pack MFI style and to cut costs his customer would assemble it himself. David was worried he wouldn't get it done as they were gathering at Ewelock Bank the next day. "Don't worry," he said, "When I've owt new I'm to catch to put to bed."

Expert waller

I was talking to one of those Breaks Hall lads and told him I'd admired their walling on the Soulby road. He explained he was only allowed to wall the inside wall as he wasn't that experienced but his cousin walled the road side. He'd had a number of excursions off the road in his car and got the relevant required practise.

MUFC milk quota

I was at a Crosby Garret customer and we were discussing milk quotas and he asked me if I was aware Manchester United held the most milk quota in the country. We agreed it must be because they milk their fans. I hasten to add I was across the beck from Chapel Farm!

Mummy's Maestro

I run a diesel Escort for my NFUing but the nature of the job means I'm never at home at a set time so the car is not available for the Brownie run, the ballet or football training run or the trip to Safeways, so I have to admit we are environmentally unfriendly and have a second car.

We obtain these gems from Mr Ashley's 'Classic Car department". That's not on the front among the new and nearly new gleaming models but round the corner mixed among the scrap and MOT failures. The last 'Classic' we acquired was an E-reg Maestro and that was over four years ago and she's a real gem. Now I'm sure poor Mr Ashley has been in

trouble before for failing old bangers' MOTs but not for getting them through their MOTs - not until now. My wife gets cross with him, every year because she fancies something a bit better but her Maestro flies through the test. Poor Roy has to keep out of her way.

The old girl keeps developing mystery illnesses - the car that is - but they seem to cure themselves when I drive her. She just won't lie down. She's developed quite a leak recently through the sun roof and you can get dripped on, especially your legs. Marian had been complaining to Mrs Ashley about it who was doing her best to interest me in a replacement. I had to disappoint her as thought a pair of leggings was a much better option. I can remember a much loved Mini pick-up I owned which had to have holes put in the floor to let the water out so we've a way to go yet!

She blows out clouds of blue smoke especially when accelerating so it's brought a new word into the family vocabulary, when some poor unfortunate gets overtaken and disappears in the blue haze, they've been "Maestroed". Mr Ashley informs me it's a highly technical system that changes it's own oil - you just keep tipping it in at the top and it keeps disappearing.

She's much more that just a car and loves to keep you guessing. When you dip your lights are they going to go out? On a cold morning do you defrost the outside or the inside first and if you pull up at a road junction will she keep running? Now Roy did say the last MOT was the LAST but touch wood we're still OK, held together with NFU and Newcastle United stickers. Marian will go daft if it sneaks through again!

How old?

I wrote last month about estimating the age of father's cows. Now he knew they were a bit long in the tooth but thought it was a bit of an insult when their documents came back showing a date of birth of 11/11/1111. He felt a bit better when I explained all cattle of indeterminable age were treated the same.

Load of bull

MY Drybeck customer was in the office insuring a bull on loan. We were completing the form, all was going well: name, address, ear no., etc., until we got to the animal's name. Now father used to have a bull that went on its holidays and the farmer who borrowed him christened him 'Thistle' for insurance purposes. He was a prickly beggar but that was nothing on this gentleman. His bull's name was Bill Clinton, I nearly fell off my chair.

Lamb pen

I still cannot understand the way farmers stand around in the alleys at the auction getting in the way but maybe I've got a clue. I was stood out of the way in one of the pens having the crack before it was time to go through when someone came past and asked if it was the wether lamb pen. Cheeky begger - I'm proven! But I'll get my own back.

DIY

WE'VE been busy getting our yows ready for the tups. We'd had to dip them with a syringe as we could get nothing worth dipping them in. I got the job of remarking them and being a softie pen pusher went home with a blister off the brush. I didn't get much sympathy at home: "You've never blistered your hand on a paint brush in the house before!" It's very true. Marian's a whiz at DIY so I leave her to it.

A new job

I don't think we've ever had as wet a back-end and our garth and pens have been full of puddle. Now Mr Rap the dog was on death's door earlier in the year so he moved into the house to recuperate and there he has stayed. The last job of the day has now changed - it's wash and dry the dog. He's not very keen yet and puts on his most hurt face.

Cheer up

I was sat at a farmhouse kitchen table and their was a *Farmer's Weekly* so I would have a quick read but realised it was a 1996 edition. The farmer's first reason for having it was the usual - he couldn't afford a new one. Then he had to admit it was to cheer himself up. Looking at what prices might get back to but also to see what the experts thought and how far out they were!

Follow the rules to the letter

I'VE seen the most sickening sight in the floods - a trailer loaded with 41 dead swaledale gimmer lambs washed down the Eden and gathered up behind a fence downstream, not very pleasant. I heard a similar tale further down the valley where some cattle had suffered a similar fate and the farmer on reading his passport regulations understood the paperwork should follow the animals. Had he to throw the passports in the Eden after them? He did well to see the funny side.

Double your money

I was asked to look at a damaged hay-bob up Stainmore. It had seen many years service and its proud owner had tried to row-in a gate-stoop with it. We were discussing on insurance value and I asked him if he knew how to double its value - fit it with a new set of tyres. I'll not tell you what Gordon called me.

Tele sales

WE all get the double glazing and time share ladies on the phone. A local farmer's wife had won a holiday (surprise, surprise) but had to answer two questions. Did they own their own home: "Yes" Did they earn more than £18,000: "No they were farmers." The line went dead!!!

A Tuesday night out

TUESDAY nights aren't quite what they were a year or two ago when lambs were a flying trade - they used to be as good as a night out. They still have their moments though when Uncle Bryan and Ted Procter start trading insults: "The Greengrass and Newsreel Show."

Cattle count 2000

I hope you have got your form filled in and sent back. I know forms are depressing but this one should make things easier once everything is on record (honest). There is a brighter side do you know where they're going to be processed - MEXICO - that's right - MEXICO. So hombre, getta your form sent back before you're locked up lika some common bandito!

1066 and all that

DECLARING the ages of cows on the form reminded me of days blood testing in years gone by. It was always November and always sleeting and every cow seemed to be eight-years-old. I can vividly remember the vets checking, asking: "Was that eight or eighteen, Morland." It was anybody's guess! In a similar vein, father tells a wonderful tale about a farm scheme for ploughing out permanent pasture where you had to state the last time the land was ploughed. He didn't think it had ever been ploughed so sent it back blank. It came back so he said not ploughed and sent it back again. It came back again so he put 1066 - that seemed to satisfy them. Things don't improve much!

The Cockermouth boys

I travelled down country to a meeting with the Cockermouth boys - Jim driving and David map reading - we went three times round a roundabout and took numerous wrong turnings. It's a wonder they ever find that fancy wigwam they call an office in Cockermouth.

Sheep demo

I attended quite an interesting demonstration on modern methods, electronic tagging, back scanning for fat and muscle and flock health, but by far the most impressive piece of tackle was not really on display - it was a mobile penning system with a race and hurdles that packed away on a trailer. The cost of one was impressive too, that impressive we'll be stuck with hurdles and string at Hause Farm for a long time to come.

Dyno-rod

I wrote about my trip to London last month. I was amused to walk past Downing Street and see a Dyno-Rod van parked up - Mr Blair having trouble with his sewerage? Well that was in August so after his problems in recent weeks with fuel, pensions, etc. he's sure to have had them in again!

Three times a day milking
THEY'RE a pretty traditional lot at Bank End, Appleby, so I was surprised to hear a neighbour saying he thought they'd gone on to three times a day milking with the cows queuing outside the parlour in the middle of the morning. It was of course a leg pull and I was getting after Andrew about his lie-in when he got his own back telling me about Jonathan, the son next door, fast asleep on the bike one morning getting the cows in. I believe he'd had a night on the tiles in true Young Farmer tradition.

Quite a day
On 20 April we had seventeen sheep left to lamb and with that few you usually expect them to lamb one every other day and stretch the agony out over a month or so. Well on 20 April we had seven out of seventeen lambed - not bad eh!

Also on the same day I was in Shap and saw they were watering the bowling green. Yes on 20 April in Shap! Any other year you would have sunk in to it over your shoes.

South country sheep - or lack of them
IN this part of the world, we think we're just about up to our ears in sheep. I've just come back from a week's holiday in Norfolk and there's not so many there. I saw more pigs than sheep and even more horses than sheep. We travelled to London one day on the train, an hour and a half trip. I was farming out of the window all the way and didn't see one sheep - no black and white cows either. We stayed on a farm - I loved the notice on his gate: "Every third rep shot and the second has just left." (NFU men aren't considered as reps, of course).

Over the hill?
WE are always being told about the increasing average age of the farming community so for any feeling the strain just remember - it's better being over the hill than under it! It fits well with the old one - Farm as if you're going to live forever and live as if you are going to die tomorrow.

Poor Uncle Jack certainly subscribed to this philosophy. When told by the doctor not that long ago it was time he slowed down and acted his age he told him he had no intention of acting his age!

Catching

WE were clipping our last few sheep and I was catching and wrapping for Eric Hornsby. He complimented me on my catching, just in the right place all the right time. It's easily explained. I've being doing it for years and had numerous serious tellings off from father if they're not quite at the right spot or quite at the right angle. Practise makes perfect!

The clipping men

In recent years we have managed our own clipping but with losing Rodger and "Anno Domini" taking its toll every year, we decided to get in the clipping men. I'd heard plenty about them so we looked no further than the Soulby gang. We can only get our labour force together at a weekend and this suited them so we fitted in nicely.

The nature of our type of sheep meant we were going to get a visit or two - the hoggs and geld yows are always ready before sucked yows, and the inside yows before the fell yows. The weather didn't help either getting rained off once or twice.

The first go to work was one damply morning when we had about 140 Cheviot hoggs housed and four of them landed to clip (Andrew Little, Geoffrey Birkbeck, Richard Balmer and Chris Cannon). Our hoggs were penned in one end of the building and one of them questioned if you could fit them in that amount of space. I said shout BOO at Cheviot hoggs and they'll fit in half as much space.

Now Can-R-Cum was in attendance as she usually is and was watching them very carefully to decide who she wanted to clip her two sheep. Speed was not taken into consideration, kindness to the sheep and lack of cuts were the two factors. Standing on their necks as they finished them off or leaving tufts were definite no-nos. After careful study she decided she wanted Decker to clip her little flock (I don't think she was too bad a judge).

Father was the pushing up man, these Cheviots had not seen a clipping trailer before so they went up no problem. I was wrapping but we enlisted the help of "Monkey" Wearmouth who reckoned he didn't know how to wrap but managed more than adequately. Four of them clipping hoggs wasn't too bad as hoggs are all clipping from their bellies right up to their ears so we kept up OK. Some of the bellies weren't too good a going as a gimmer or two turned out to be wethers... much to the clippers' amusement!

The next time they came they apologised as disaster had struck as there were only two of them. Andrew was assisting with the birth of his second child although the general opinion was he wouldn't be much help and Chris was silaging. Monkey and I didn't think it was a disaster, four of them peeling yows off would be more than hectic. This was much more civilised. I don't know why but they seemed to take great pleasure out of seeing me sweat. I didn't disappoint as I can sweat at the thought of work. I never got Monkey told we weren't as well organised as his father - in his clipping shed the most important piece of gear seems to be a deck chair.

I thought I knew all about clipping equipment, machines and cables, combs, cutters and hand pieces, but apparently the most important part of equipment is the mobile phone, the front of their Land Rover was full of them. I'd never seem anyone clipping whilst holding a conversation on a mobile before. It looked much more dangerous than driving and talking.

The other piece of gear father wasn't too keen on was Andrew's ghetto blaster - he offered to blast it with his hammer and was more relieved when it didn't come out when Andrew was absent.

The way the summer went within two days Monkey the wool wrapper became Monkey the baler leader ably assisted by "Bob the Builder" Mason. Can he mew them - YES HE CAN. If you have no idea what I'm prattling on about you obviously don't watch kiddies TV - ask someone who does.

Embarrassed

AS I said in the previous bit, Andrew Little missed clipping because he was attending his daughter's birth. A couple of years later I had Rachel in the office who told me in a large voice, in front of quite a few customers: "I always think of you when it's my daughter's birthday."

Mad

POOR Bob came back from Turkey and 47C of heat in the morning and was leading bales that night. Bob reckoned he was either hard-up or mad to be hay timing. Paying good money to be cooked at 47C, Monkey and I thought he either had too much money or was mad. Draw your own conclusions!

Missing mutton

THINGS went well. We got hay timed and clipped, the lads from Soulby made a good job and the crack was good, the sheep were as tidy, and there was no more mutton missing than if we had done them ourselves.

More things you see when you haven't got a camera

I was travelling from Tebay to Newbiggin and could have taken a picture to sum up silage time (up to late June anyway). Rain was starting to spot the car windscreen and there was Jimmy standing next to his tractor and strowing up machine, cap in one hand, scratching his head with the other and looking up to the heavens. I'm not sure whether he was looking for inspiration or divine intervention, but all he would get was WET.

Hay timing

WHAT a wonderful week, brilliant weather and for once brilliantly forecast. Our problem was not the weather but whether our old tackle would hold together. The only casualties were ten broken hay-bob tynes, two baler shear bolts and a peeling sunburnt nose, so we had a good do.

A tight fit

WE had a meeting down at Skelmersdale and I had some large signs to collect, so arranged to borrow father's Toyota pick-up. I was amused when I was contacted by the Kendal office to see if I could give Chris Davies and Sarah a lift back. Now Chris is put together on similar lines to myself so that doesn't leave much room for Sarah. Can-R-Cum can still just about squeeze her bum between the seats, but on close inspection I don't think Sarah could quite manage. They made other arrangements.

Think tank

DID you see Channel 4's programme about farming - *A Dying Breed*? It was mainly good stuff- my favourite bit was the slurry tanker with GOVERNMENT THINK TANK painted on it.

A slow down

I was running wind off last month about how seven out of our last seventeen yows to lamb, lambed in one day. It didn't continue - in the next fortnight only five of the remaining ten managed to give birth!

Too fast

WE'VE been riding over Orton Scar on a regular basis and been busy watching them calving at Bank Head. To the kids' delight there's a Belted Galloway and it hadn't calved and they were keen to know if it would have a beltie calf. I had the proud owner in and asked him. "Unfortunately," he said, "it had been 'a bulling' the day before so wouldn't be calving." He bought it as 'run with bull' but it must have been running too fast.

Hogg wintering

OUR hoggs didn't get away to winter until January because of all the problems with licences and the like, but their holiday was extended a month to the end of April and what a difference it made. They were a pretty motley crew when they went, but they came back different sheep. Father had given grandson, James, a gimmer lamb with a coloured face so he could "ken" it. It was a pretty poor affair. He called it "Floppy" because its ear hung down the side of its head.

Well, when we got them back we had to go through them a couple of times before we could be sure which one it was. Floppy was at least twice as big, with pricked ears and fit to race.

I'd like to quote the lowland farmer here who told me these hill farmers should really be paid to fetch their sheep down the valley to tidy up their farms - but he'd kill me.

The milk price

THE derisory price of milk has been well publicised and I was discussing the matter with someone who's gone back in after foot and mouth and was uplifted by his attitude: "I might be milking cows just to amuse myself but if I did mek out it would be before main o'folk got up."

Cash or grass

YOU know what the price of store cattle's like. I was told if a farmer has plenty of grass and plenty of cash, the grass will not be wasted!

Will he get in?

I was walking into a DEFRA meeting at Carlisle with County Chairman, Will, and we were discussing writing in the NFU magazine and he expressed his surprise I hadn't had a go at him. Well, I have to tell you he was attempting to gain access to DEFRA's offices with Wendy Harrison's pass around his neck and it had her photo on it. It won't surprise you to hear he successfully got past the security men. It begs the question, does this mean he's a big girl's blouse?

The good the bad and the ugly

Last month's magazine had hardly dropped through the letter box when I received my first call about the cover picture (reproduced on page 57). There was a mistake - it should have been subtitled "The good the bad and the ugly". My mate Mr Pigney thought Alan Alderson was OK, he didn't think much of Dr Iain Anderson so you know which category I fell in! You know what they say about people in glass houses.

Speaking of Mr Pigney I thought I was going to have a claim off him, I jumped off his bike to catch a yow and it gave me a tremendous electric shock - a right belt up the back of my leg. But I was wrong, not being the finely tuned athlete I once was I'd forgotten about hamstrings and that's what I'd done, torn a hamstring - OUCH!

Good lads

I was praising our tups at scanning time but they'd done even better than we thought. They escaped at the beginning of November and loused themselves so we're lambing at the start of April among all the sunny weather instead of waiting for the weather to break in the second half of the month. With less old yows, a bit of grass and sunshine it's made life much pleasanter.

In previous years we've numbered our twin lambs and spent hours mothering them up. This year we gave up numbering them as it was a waste of time. The biggest problem has been the old beggars mothering lambs up for hours before they lamb themselves. Don't get me wrong, I'm not trying to be a clever so and so and tell you we had no disasters it was just easier than sometimes.

Names

THE twins we did mark were lettered as the kids like to give them names. The As were Adam and Annabel and I remember the Vs were Veronica and Victor. The Ss were the best - Shearer and Solano, what a combination. We've had Barbara a little smart Cheviot pet gimmer from Raisgill Hall and there was also Dopey Donald. He came into the world very slowly with a leg back and didn't speed up much. He spent the first two hours mothering himself on to a gate stoop while his mother did laps of the field at a tremendous rate of knots. He spent the next few days lying flat to the ground making us all think he'd passed away but he's still with us despite doing a wonderful impersonation of a rabbit and disappearing down a rabbit hole with only his back feet sticking out.

Baby Bob

BOB Mason who helps us had an addition to his own family last year and after landing late one evening had decided it was easier suckling lambs than babies as "Baby Bob" wouldn't suck. You couldn't kick its backside and put it back in the pen with its mother either.

Highly trained

ALL NFU Group Secretaries and their staff in the county have been trained in recent weeks on making insurance sales and the regulations that go with it. Tina went to Penrith for her day off and when asked to comment on the training said: "You can't teach an old dog new tricks." I wouldn't have dared call her an old dog!

I went down to Kendal and the first thing we had to do was write our names as a name plate (wonderful isn't it!) Chris Davis down there wrote Richard Gere on his - the speed he moves at we thought it should have been "Bottom Gear".

In ten or fifteen years I will be fully trained and they will want to pension me off.

Monday, 4 March

MONDAY, 4 March was the first live auction in Kirkby Stephen following foot and mouth, and I was just like a lot of others and went along to see what went on and I guess just check it actually happened. I wouldn't say folk were actually going around cuddling each other, but the atmosphere was certainly uplifting and the most optimistic I've seen for some time. Now whether we've any right to be optimistic is open to question but it was definitely a nice way to spend an hour or two.

DAFTA survey

FATHER was asked to complete a DAFTA questionnaire and reluctantly agreed an official could visit the farm and he answered their queries which he reckoned would be of little use - then what happened, two or three days later - DAFTA rang back and wanted to come and do the same questionnaire again. Some things don't improve!

Another local farmer was asked to do this and on questioning the DAFTA official further was told it was to find out how he kept his farm clear of foot and mouth in the "Penrith Spur". He quickly told them it was because he kept buggers like him off the farm and put the phone down.

Starting lambing

WHEN we scanned, Adrian warned us we had a yow that would lamb early - we had guessed because she ran with the tups all summer. Anyway, he was right as you can see from the photograph on page 59. We've had plenty of mornings with six inches of snow or when we've been about under water, but she had lambed on the most spring like morning so far this year - poor old lass, the foot and mouth must have confused her and put her off her natural instincts.

S-tags

WE were starting to think we were going to have to breed sheep with four lugs or those continental goaty things with floppy ears half way down to their knees, so we could accommodate all the tags DAFTA were going to make us use. I am sure you will have seen by now a lot of them, especially for wintering sheep, can be replaced by paint marks. This was the powers that be's efforts to push us down the road of individual tagging for sheep and I personally, think the NFU have done very well to hit it on the head and so quickly. As with a lot of restriction following foot and mouth, I hope to see us get them lifted at a sensible pace as the year goes on.

Scanning again

SCANNING was the last ordinary job we did last year before foot and mouth struck and we've just been on again. I wrote at tupping time and said we were left with 270 yows and nine tups so we weren't expecting many geld yows. Well as the most eloquent of Manchester United footballers would say "The boys dun great" - 7 geld, 134 singles, 126 twins and four sets of triplets.

Our scanning was a bit early this year because we couldn't move our tups so they loused themselves. We normally get Adrian as he's easing off but this year tupping and lambing are all over the place. As he said he hasn't scanned a sheep that's been farmed as it should have been in the last twelve months. I wonder how it will effect the lamb trade come back-end.

Wet, wet, wet

I watched the weather on 11 February and they said there'd been ten inches of rain in Shap in February - an inch of rain a day - no wonder it's been a bit damp underfoot. There's one thing about ten inches of rain at Shap - it's soon down the hill and someone else's problem.

Photo opportunity

I wasn't invited to see Mrs Beckett when she did her Cumbria Farm Visits. I can't think why. But I do have it on good authority she only had one real clear aim at these farm visits - NOT to have her photo taken with a cow. I can't think why!

Mobile madness

POOR Uncle Bryan was getting upset and perturbed because everyone kept calling him "The Fat Man". He couldn't weigh it up at all until someone advised him to ring his own mobile phone, which, of course, you wouldn't normally do. When he did, he found his message said something along the lines of: "This is the Fat Man here, but I'm asleep. Leave your name and number and I'll get back when I eventually wake up." Cousin Ian will cop it when he gets back off his holidays.

Two good things

FOOT and mouth has caused me nothing but a lot of work and hassle but it did strike me the other day there's perhaps two good things to come out of it. I've got the best pair of leggings I've ever had courtesy of DAFTA and come lambing time, although we'll miss the sport, we have no Cheviot shearlings to chase - the poor beggars were put in a hole at Great Orton back in April.

The Sun

I now have a real claim to fame being quoted on page 2 of *The Sun* on the 1st January. An excited young lady from regional office at Skelmersdale rang me up to tell me about it and wondered if there was a picture of me sitting on the quad bike with no clothes on. I had to tell her no and if there was it would be pretty disappointing and as hard as the

Page 3 material?

weather was over the New Year it would be more than disappointing! The best part was my new position, I was referred to as "National Farmers' Union Chief Mike Sanderson." I wonder if anyone's told the regional director yet? I was soon brought down to earth by Peter Allen MBE (Many Beers Enjoyed) who suggested the printing was poor and it really was NFU chef, he obviously knows nothing about my cooking.

F&M 'all clear' joy on farms

By ROBIN PERRIE

BRITAIN was declared free of foot-and-mouth last night — apart from one county set to be given the all-clear within days.

A flock of 2,100 sheep were slaughtered in **NORTHUMBERLAND** as a precaution.

But vets insist the county will lose its "at risk" status soon.

Britain can then apply to restart animal exports.

The ban has cost the industry £12million-a-week since the outbreak began in February — the total bill for the crisis is estimated at **£6BILLION**.

More than four million animals have been killed and up to 7,800 farming jobs lost. Thousands more were put out of work in tourism.

Charges

National Farmers' Union chief Mike Sanderson said: "I don't think we've ever looked forward to a New Year like this but there is still a long way to go."

Restrictions were lifted on Durham, North Yorks and Cumbria.

Sunday marked the 90-day safety threshold since the last outbreak at Little Asby, Cumbria.

Farm owner Lydia Watson, 72, said: "It's a great relief it's over."

Bobby Waugh, 55, still faces charges after his pig farm in Heddon-on-the-Wall, Northumberland, was suspected as the origin of the outbreak.

Good news and bad news

WE have a few good lads who help us on the farm when we're busy but the main man is Bob Mason. He's also a keen hunting man. Father had arranged with him to land one Saturday morning when we had a bit on. He then rang father up a day or two before and he told him he had some good news and some bad news. Father got the good news first and that was the hunting started again on Saturday, father told him he needn't bother him with the bad news!

Ring my bell

I'VE never told my favourite foot & mouth story here. My rugby mate Willie farms at Edenhall and is extremely proud of his thriftiness, we even have a bell at the club that is rung if he buys a round. I can assure you there is plenty of wear left in it. Poor Willie went down with FMD early on. We heard about it on the grapevine but his name never appeared on the telly or on the internet for quite a while. My kids who spend a bit of time at the rugby club with me know of his reputation and wondered if you had to pay to get your name included.

Moving the right way (slowly)

IT seems an age since we lost our sheep on the fell but we finally got some turned back this last day or so (20 January) and it does look good although every now again you see one out of the corner of your eye and think it shouldn't be there. Nearly every time I go out now I see livestock in a field I've not seen any in for months. We're getting there slowly.

Logic

I'VE said all along there's been no logic in all of this lot. I've even had it confirmed by officials in DAFTA, but footpaths and sentinels take the biscuit. If you have sentinels there's a list of rules several pages long, you're virtually a prisoner on your farm yet walkers are at liberty to walk through your stock, then through your neighbour's stock and then through his neighbours, crazy or what? As is the norm with foot and mouth the answer is politics.

Something to talk about

I was leaving a meeting that lasted a good hour longer than it should have done and was complaining bitterly when a wise old head told me: "Some people go to meetings with something to say and others just have to say something." - Indeed!

Road side rescue

YOU have got to smile - as you will know if you lose a cow over 30 months old the Ministry will pick it up free of charge to inspect its brain. You will probably get them to pick up sheep as well as they don't seem to know the difference! Well, my part time farmer and NFU member/Ford man across the road needed to use this service and asked if I could get him the telephone number. I did, and quoted him 0800 252890 and he rang back shortly afterwards convinced I was taking the "Michael".

He'd got a roadside rescue service and they could do something for his car but not his cow. It tickled me and I wished I had thought of it myself. The correct number is 0800 525890 for removal of cows so make a note of it for future use. I still haven't convinced him it was a mistake.

First time ever

I don't know if it's what the bird people and environmentalists planned. but for the first time in living memory we have magpies at Hause Farm. Great, if you're a Newcastle supporter but not so good for most of the other wildlife.

Above, the Good, the Bad and the Ugly and below, Mr. Rap's car

Above New Fair mess and below, the author

Above, 'No slow lambs, no quick lambs, only dead lambs' and sign of hope, first twins, Below, Kevin Alderson's painting.

Tessa, Floppy and Pop-eye

Tina Turner on the last day and below wall covering...

Above, the Full Monty and below, doing a turn with the old baler

Above Can-R-Go, Rap and Glen. Below sale day at Hause Farm

Above, snacker feed system and below the demo in London.

Nameless

ONE farmer who must remain nameless, was collecting his "Sole Occupational Licence" from the vet and asked what it allowed him to do. "Nothing you haven't been doing already," was the reply.

Hill tup

I was admiring a young farmer's vehicle at Shap who is very keen on his sheep. His registration number was something like H11 TUP. I told him I suppose he had to have that as there's too many letters in wether.

When is a bite not a bite

Our dog has been poorly. He was to pill and father couldn't make a thing of him. No problem I thought, I'll hold his mouth open while father pokes the pill down his throat. I ended up with a very badly bitten finger but insisted the dog hadn't bitten me - he'd just shut his mouth while my hand was in it. My Missus just laughed at me and told me he'd bitten me.

A welcome visitor

WHILE recovering Mr Rap has been getting 5 star treatment and living in the house. Dad and Mam had a weekend off so I took him back to Appleby with me for the evening - and he had a marvellous time. Put the cat to flight and ate its supper. had two piddles in the kitchen and numerous more in the backyard along with another more substantial deposit, rove a dustbin bag to bits and covered the house in dog hair. He hasn't been invited back!

Oil seed rape?

DID you go up Mallerstang in late June? If you did you'll no doubt be wondering if they're going to change its name to Buttercup Valley. I don't think I've ever seen as many buttercups. I guess it's a mixture of the spring and summer we've had so far and the ESA, environmentalists must like buttercups!

Appleby New Fair - an alternative view

OUR travelling friends have come and gone for another year and if previous years' press coverage is anything to go by, we'll see pictures of black and white horses being washed in the river, colourful picturesque hooped caravans, cherubs sitting on the steps of caravans with lurcher dogs and a wonderful time had by all.

The actual truth is somewhat different with filth, mess and litter being the more apt subjects. Most of what goes on, is not fit to print but suffice to say the number of toilet facilities in no way match the number of 'visitors' and as it does, nature takes its course, sometimes in the most unusual ways.

This year has seen a diversion from the norm, with an encampment appearing on a couple of occasions on Crosby Ravensworth Common. If you follow the local press.you'll have seen the common mentioned in recent weeks because of visits from people of real importance at the ministry because of the fell's status and importance to the environment. It was something of a contradiction of terms to see it ploughed up and covered in gas bottles, litter and plastic - and goodness only knows what else on closer inspection, but I drove past and didn't investigate any further.

Goodness only knows what would have happened if a local farmer had done something a tenth as bad as that. In the local press the English Nature spokesman said as much - they'd have jumped on the farmer from a great height, but couldn't deal with the traveller - now there's a surprise - but I suppose they're not the only ones who only go for the soft targets.

Looking out of my office, I overlook the bridge in Appleby over the Eden and can see the police on duty. One lunch time I watched the sport and saw a worker at the local pizza shop get a parking ticket, two drivers of cars with local registration plates got a lecture about not wearing their seat belts and a chrome covered pick-up full of kids standing in the back went past with barely a second glance.

I must praise Eden District Council for their efforts at cleaning - every morning the centre of Appleby is returned to some sort of normality after the previous evening's 'going ons' and trails of chip papers, cans, bottles. cartons, etc. Their efforts on Orton Scar were also to be commended, but of course, its us that pay the rates and the wages. But after that, they do it very well.

So there you have it. Under siege in your own home town. every journey and every little thing you need to do, for a week you have to give great thought to. You've the muck, the mess and the smell to put up with - and we all pay for the privilege - see picture on page 58.

Faith

ON 30 April we had a yow scanned geld produce a lamb. Can-R-Cum was in attendance and confidently informed me it was my fault for marking it wrong as the scanning man doesn't make mistakes. Isn't it wonderful when your children have such faith in you! Not the scanning man's fault of course!

Our old dog

I was cracking our old dog up last month catching Cheviot shearlings but he's had a savage lambing time. We had a weekend marking lambs out and on the Monday and Tuesday night he could hardly go at all. We were quite bothered about him and I said to father I thought more about that dog than some folk. Then I decided I was wrong - There's not many folk I think more about than our larl dog. It's just a shame he's like the rest of us and gets a year older each year.

Finished lambing

THE horrors of lambing time have been the main point of discussion with most of my visitors recently. I asked one hill man if he'd finished lambing. He said the yows might not have but he had - he'd had a bellyful.

First cut

We've successfully completed our first cut at Shap - chased the yows out of the meadows. A wonderful job they made of it as well. I was right behind them with the manure drill and couldn't see a thing. It was that bad I had father on the bike on the previous time round as a guide. He got a few funny looks by one or two driving past. He's a bit sharp - I was trying to splatter him on the comers and the row ends but he managed to keep out of the way - most of the time!

A pain in the neck and elsewhere

I don't see why only half the local population should be amused by my misfortune, so I thought I might as well share it with the rest. Can anyone explain why with most illnesses and ailments you get a reasonable amount of sympathy, but when its anything to do with your bottom everyone thinks it's hilarious.

I've had a boil up my backside and was doing a very passable impersonation of John Wayne walking down Dodge City after seven hard days in the saddle - sitting down was a tricky manoeuvre and getting into the car was worse. Some things were worse than that but I won't go into detail, as I know the gentile nature of the readers of this publication.

I'd been to the doctors twice, which to anyone who knows me shows how bad it was. On the second visit, he sent me to Carlisle Infirmary to get the offending item drained. Little did I, or the doctor realise all I was short of, was a swift ride to Carlisle with the wife driving through every pothole and over every cat's eye. I got out of the car in the Infirmary car park and my waters had broken, either that or I had lost control of my bowels.

Within minutes, relief overtook me - wonderful! We still went ahead and saw the consultant, 'Mack the Knife'. It eventually dawned on me what he wanted to do - take his knife and wreak havoc in my nether regions. I had been offered an alternative operation privately the day before in H. Pigney & Sons. Something to do with bending over a desk and a Stanley knife and to be honest it seemed by far the better choice.

With lambing only a day or two away, the thought of being laid up for a fortnight could not really be contemplated so I had to politely explain my position and refuse his kind offer to put me through all kinds of agony. I stand a chance of the condition recurring but touch wood - so far so good. So after all that, I was lucky enough to be able to go lambing.

Coming out

AFTER coming out last month with my medical problem, I think I've had the most feedback and certainly the most giggles over anything I have ever written. You'd be amazed how many folk have sympathised because they had suffered something similar - there's also plenty of others offered me their own home-made cure and very painful most of them sound.

Lucky

I am not sure whether I was lucky or not to be going lambing with the weather and a bit of abortion among our shearlings we have had a really tatty time. Sitting having your breakfast knowing the next job is to catch four Cheviot shearlings in 8O acres is not too relaxing. But catch them we did - Mr Rap sitting on the bike is still up to it at twelve or thirteen -

Shows what a life times hard work and a good cursing every day can do for you.

Good for the Soul
THERE'S a man out of Shap often walks his old sheepdog on the fell and it doesn't bother father because it's too old and too fat to do any harm. Father was gathering the fell and had Rap on the bike. He stopped and talked to the man and asked him how old his old dog was. The man said: "He's eight and doing well for his age." Father pointed out his dog was at least twelve and a hell of an advert for hard work.

Nail biting
THE school Easter holidays were a godsend as Can-R-Cum has been able to help. She's certainly more than useful although she's been on edge as seventeen days have come and gone and her two black sheep still haven't lambed. She's always getting into trouble for biting her nails, but has managed to overcome the problem - her hands have always been covered in something disgusting and she couldn't face biting them.

Pet lambs
WE'VE been laiting pet lambs here, there and everywhere and someone was worried when I was putting some in the footwell of father's pick-up they might make a mess. I told them not to worry - the dog would eat it next time he got in.

Credit where credit's due
WITH my aforementioned medical problem, lambing and the Easter holidays I was missing from the office for the best part of three weeks and things were still running smoothly on my return. It must show either how little I do or how good the staff is - thanks Tina.

Dip disposal
IT'S nice to have some victories and anyone who paid their £107 dipping disposal charge should be just about getting their money back.

Up to their bellies

SOMEONE was telling me they had seen some sheep up to their bellies in grass - I told them ours were, but only because their feet had sunk a foot into the clart.

Knocking off time

A Drybeck farmer had a very earnest young man from the ministry doing an IACS inspection. He had spent two whole days going round all the fields measuring everything in sight from heaps of big bales to middens and lanes. He landed into the yard at 5.30pm on the second day with sheaves of papers wanting to discuss all his discrepancies, which probably would be lucky if they amounted to half an acre. The farmer however was sorry to advise him he shut at five o'clock and he would have to come back at nine in the morning.

Thermal windows

TINA took a telephone call and told me there was someone from Thermal Windows wanted to talk to me. I'd never even heard of thermal windows before. I must be going deaf in my old age. It was Thelma Winder. It did give us a good giggle and we've called her Thermal ever since.

Tongue tied

I was amused by one of my customers who was after British Telecom and wanted the name of their customer relations officer. The poor girl on the phone had a bad lisp and apologised before she started. The name she wanted was Mrs S Sixsmith, try saying that with a lisp!

Rich man poor man

I was in a farmhouse kitchen when a visitor asked us what the difference was between a rich farmer and a poor farmer? The poor farmer washes his own Mercedes! He beat a hasty retreat. I hasten to add he wasn't an agricultural type rep. He should have looked outside - the farmer had an F-reg Volvo.

Did you hear the one about the young woman walking past the well when she heard cries of help from it. She rescued a frog from the bottom of the well who promised he was a farmer with a 500 acre farm and if she kissed him he would turn back into a farmer and marry her. She put the frog in her pocket. "Are you not going to kiss me?"

"No," she replied, "a talking frog's worth more than any farmer I know."

Patience

I am writing this in the relative calm of mid-March but it is now mid-April and all hell has broken loose. Please be patient with us. All IACS forms and extensification queries will be dealt with, once I've completed my lambing break. We had a decent scan so we know they're all in there, it's just the next stage, getting them out. I do hope it is nice and sunny and mild.

Brown, Blair and chocolate eclairs

THE NFU AGM is now long gone and you will have heard all the political goings on. I was fortunate (or unfortunate) enough to be invited and will share some of the lighter moments you won't have read about.

I was definitely in the hall at the time but right at the side and I didn't see the eclair business until I got home and saw it on the telly. My wife was convinced I was in the bar - at best.

Peter Allen our LFA man spends a lot of time in London with all the work he does down there and looked after some of us less well travelled peasants. He found us somewhere not too dear to eat, but the beer down there is dreadfully expensive. Mind, we always seemed to find somewhere at Cumbrian prices when it was his turn to pay!

I'm not sure if our County Chairman, Harold Armstrong will include his favourite moment in his notes. Standing having a piddle only to be joined by Franz Fischler.

There are two schools of thought on the way forward with Mr. Blair, the first being he's just turned up to keep us quiet, his talk of partnership and a way forward is just 'spin' and the best course of action is outright confrontation. Heckle and boo him and instead of the afore mentioned eclair a large bucket of manure would be much more appropriate. We've nothing to lose as we'll get nothing out of him anyway and we might as well blockade the ports and have a ride down the M6 with a fleet of tractors. Whether this would be the right or wrong approach it would certainly give great pleasure in the short term and make my job a lot easier.

The second school of thought is that the chances are we will have to put up with New Labour for at least another seven years and it is a long time. If we go for Downing Street or the Ministry of Agriculture and rant and rave and get the door locked behind us as we leave how do we influence policy and politics for next seven years? We are constantly reminded of what the Tories did to the mining industry and I'm sure they'd be plenty in the Labour Party happy to see farming suffer now the boot is on the other foot.

I'm not sure which theory I subscribe to myself as both arguments have merit perhaps somewhere in between is the best plan with the grass-roots men opting for option one and those up in London who have to deal with the powers that be going mainly for the second.

I wasn't impressed with much Nick Brown said but he did say he had heard it said the NFU was in the Minister's pocket. He then went on to say in the Cabinet they think it's the other way round.

I also heard William Hague speak and he came over very well. We could have whatever we wanted as soon as he was in power - dead easy isn't it! It sounded as if the NFU had written his speech for him, in fact there was a whisper it had!

I wouldn't read too much into the chocolate eclair stunt as it seemed just a bit of a coincidence that the infuriated lady in question had a portfolio of glamourous photos ready as soon as the press took an interest.

I think I as most unimpressed with Sebastian Coe who was with Hague. I expected a fine figure of a man but he was small and humpy backed. He certainly didn't look like the world-beater he undoubtedly was.

There was then the argument about being better off in the countryside. That largely depends on how you define countryside. If it's those who earn a living off the land and those others traditionally affiliated with them then Mr Blair is way off his eggs. If you're talking about everyone who doesn't live in the city well that's a totally different matter - but where does the wealth come from? Certainly not the countryside.

I've recently been down the M6 below Birmingham and coming home didn't have ten yards of clear road in front of me for the first 100 miles. Spending time in London it beats me how you can be six foot tall and a substantial three foot wide and still seem to be totally invisible to the city dwellers. When you've got to be among all those folk and pay those silly prices and be pushed from pillar to post perhaps the countryside's not too bad. As long as they keep the politicians in the city.

We came back on the train and I got off at Penrith and came across one of my customers, Keith Hall in the station car park who runs a taxi business out of Reagill. It took me quite a while on the telephone next morning to convince him my car was parked in the NFU car park and I hadn't used a rival taxi firm.

Plastic

HAVE you got any plastic wrap silage sheets, etc., you cannot get shot of? Note on 22/23 March there will be a collection at Kirkby Stephen Auction - cost £10-30 depending on the size of trailer. Not as cheap as a box of matches but better than the fine.

Electronic tagging

I was on a farm where they were putting these fancy electronic tags in their cattle. I was surprised to learn you have got to be within a couple of feet to read them. I always thought the idea was you had a radar gun and could get a number out of a Limmy bullock's ear half a field away along with its speed in miles per hour.

MAFF sheep book

EVERYONE will have got a fancy sheep record book from MAFF. In my and others' opinions within the NFU, it goes way over the top and I think the best advice is to stick with only the running total of yows and gimmer hoggs once they're twelve months old. I was looking carefully at their recommended way of completing the book and believe if you or I had done it like them, we would have been penalised.

Getting old

LAST month's notes were written prior to Christmas so this is the first chance I've had to tell you Santa brought me a cap to keep my head warm. On a Tuesday night at Kirkby Auction, very good it is as well even if I get a bit of stick. I suppose that's a sign of ageing as I need it to make up for my lack of hair but worse than that my daughter disowns me when I wear it.

MBE

CONGRATULATIONS to my colleague Nick Utting up at Carlisle who has been awarded the MBE. The rest of us mere mortal Group Secretaries have been pondering just what MBE stands for. Mad Bad &

Evil was suggested as was Mr Big Ed or even Most Bold Ego. Or was it Mr Blair's Eulogy or Mr Blair's Eunoch. It was also said a CBE might have been more appropriate Cumbria's Biggest Embarrassment or if you work in the Carlisle Office - Carlisle's Bloody Eyatolla (spelling never was my strong suit!)

I was very impressed with the newspaper coverage and even cut the article out. The picture replaced Andy Cole on my son's dart board. In all seriousness Nick well done - but you didn't expect me to miss an opportunity like this.

Ode to Europe

I came across this in the Sunday paper and. it just about sums up our continental cousins! Germany makes the rules, Britain obeys the rules, France bends the rules, Spain breaks the rules, Greece and Italy don't know there are any rules.

Caught out

ONE sunny January afternoon I was in a farm kitchen and was being dazzled by the sun. The farmer's wife pulled the curtains so I could see what I was doing. After a while there was an almighty knock on the window and her husband was peering in wondering what was going on and then accused me of having my shirt hanging out.

Tax efficient

I was recently consulting my accountant (Cousin Paul) and we were discussing ways of reducing my tax liability. At this stage I should extol the virtues of an NFU Mutual Pension Plan or tell you about the excellent performance of an NFU Mutual ISA but we came up with a much more efficient way of avoiding tax - TAKE A FARM.

The other methods mentioned are to be recommended and I would be more than happy to arrange them for you.

Dipping fee

I have spoken to many of you about the .£107 bill for dip disposal and I'd love to be able to follow it up and tell you not to pay it. Unfortunately, it will be to pay if you want to carry on disposing of dip. In fact this fee covers April 1999 to 2000 and later in the year they will be back for another bite. We have had the man from the Environment

Agency speaking to us and I asked him why he wasn't wearing his mask. He gave me a funny look so I explained he was considered to be a bandit.

Older and wiser?

WELL, here are my first ramblings of the new Millennium or perhaps more relevant the final efforts of my first ten years as the NFU man in Appleby. I started on 1 February 1990 and have survived the first ten years. I'm certainly older, but I am not sure about wiser and there is rather more of me but rather less hair than there was in 1990. It hasn't been a bad ten years - it's just gone in a whizz!

Market research

I was settling down after eating my Sunday dinner following a very late Saturday night courtesy of Appleby Fire Service - I was at their dinner, not being rescued! Unfortunately, my chair is beside the phone and just as I was getting my feet up it rang. Some firm wanted to do some market research. I had to inform them I was far too busy going to sleep to be bothered with them.

Cow punching

FATHER is about out of cattle but still has half a dozen cows and assorted stirks. There were six heifers aged from 18 to 28 months to go and I spent quite a while on a Sunday afternoon sorting out passports, filling in the auction slip and the like. I gave father a hand on the Thursday to get them in and load them and even though they had hardly been handled in their lives, Thursday was easier than Sunday.

The drover at Penrith Auction hadn't got the job weighed up when he ventured among them with his stick. He soon beat a hasty retreat and left me to sort them!

Licensed

FATHER is 70 this month and got heaps of paperwork about renewing his driving licence. He has to have his photo taken and fill numerous forms in. Their forms can compete with MAFF's for being bad to follow. He would have me have a look at them. I asked him if he realised they'd take his licence off him if he was caught doing under 30 mph. He believed me for a minute! We couldn't find the clause where you get your licence revoked if you were caught meandering up the middle of the road looking over the dykes doing everyone else's farming for them.

The final round-up

IN mid-December we had the final sort up among our lambs. So many were fit to go to Kirkby fat and the rest went to Penrith as store. The Tuesday was pretty wintery but father got his stores sold at Penrith OK but left the rest at Kirkby and gave me instructions I had to sell them which is most unusual. He reckoned he'd struggled to get home in the snow and it had nothing to do with the fact there were the sweepings-up and he didn't want to be seen in the ring with them - I'm not so sure. Mind, we got our name in the *Herald* for them the week after, so it couldn't have been too bad.

Time flies

WHEN I was a youth all these old fuddy duddies used to talk about time flying and you used to think silly old beggars - but I tell you what - it comes to you. The years do just fly by.

Speeding

WHEN I get my car back after the weekend I am quite used to the radio being returned, the seats being moved and all the controls being fiddled with. Monday morning I was travelling down the M6 to a meeting at Skelmersdale and never checked the time till I got on the motorway at Tebay. I was running way behind time and I cannot abide being late, so I absolutely flew. It was pointed out to me later, my car clock was running 15 minutes fast so if some nice police camera man took my picture down the M6 a certain ten-year-old's drop box will be getting emptied.

Dipped up

I passed my dipping test prior to April 1998 before they dreamt up the practical test and recently received a letter which appeared to tell me I had to take a practical test. Now having read the letter very carefully several times, it doesn't actually say that, it just advises you to, so don't be misled by them.

Sign of the times
I wrote last year about Can-r-Cum getting 30p for her black fleece and having to put 20p to it to get her yow clipped. Well that was nothing - this year she cleared a whole 3p - that might just about be about enough to get its tail clipped out ready for the tup.

Canoe rescue service
ONE very windy Sunday, a couple knocked on the farm door - would we put their canoe up. They were travelling down the M6 with it strapped to the top of a van and it was like a sail and they'd about taken off. So father took pity on them and took charge of the large blue plastic canoe. After they had picked it up on a calm day, they left a bit of luck. There's one thing for certain, bed and breakfast for canoes sure beats clipping black sheep.

A poser for you
WOULD any farmer be daft enough to buy back wool at a price greatly inflated above the price he received for his own? Well I found one - Maurice Hall. I even helped load it on his trailer for him. It was woollen loft insulation. It would probably have been a lot cheaper to toss a few fleeces on the loft to keep the heat in but I guess the smell and the rats would not have been acceptable.

Skittered
WE'VE been very pleased with the way our lambs have done this back-end (apart from the price) except for one aspect. They really have been skittered, and that is being polite. We've spent hours and hours and hours clipping lamb back-sides and as father eloquently puts it: "It wouldn't be so bad if they were worth summat!" It's just a plain job cleaning them up and it doesn't help when you feel you're giving them away.

Auto-pilot
WE'VE a couple of fields down Shap and went to sort up some fat lambs. By the time we'd got the pens fastened together with string and old hur-dles, you know the kind of thing, the dog had just about got the lambs gathered up. On our return, I was telling father and his only comment was, it was just as well we didn't put the pen at the other end of the field or it might have taken an hour.

Good luck

I was pleased to get the contract to supply tup insurance at the big Swaledale sales at Kirkby Stephen. My favourite moment was quoting a price for a tup worth a few thousands but the farmer had never insured one before and didn't think he'd bother. As he left the mart office I wished him good luck. He returned after a couple of minutes and had changed his mind and he blamed me! If I had not wished him good luck he would never have thought about it again.

Milk madness

I'VE had to stand a bit of stick recently after being on Border TV and in the *Herald* promoting free school mile into Appleby Primary School. I was even presented with a pint of milk when I went to the local pub.

It actually came over well in the media but the actual story was a bit different. The free milk arrived after the cameras had left. We pinched the pre-school kiddies milk! And when the free milk was examined it got worse. It was long-life flavoured milk supplied by Lancashire Dairies - packed in the EU - and French, yes French, it beggars belief.

Whinning

LOCAL dairy farmer's wife Carol Barker had been instrumental in getting the milk and she went ballistic (quite rightly) when the source of the milk was discovered. She was busy telling me all about it in the farm kitchen when husband Neil piped up: You don't seem to mind drinking that French wine. I had to laugh but I guess it will be Australian or Chilean wine now.

Dutch courage

I received a letter from four Dutch girls wanting lambing experience between the middle of March and the first of April. According to their c.v.s they're all born in 1980 and have hobbies ranging from disco dancing to riding. Does anyone want a hand Father was quite keen but we don't start lambing until 14 April 2000 and he found out too late to lowse his tups early!

Is this you?

I was in the auction recently discussing the 'pros' and 'cons' of dressing up mule gimmer lambs and had it explained to me that a good lamb is always a good lamb but a bit of work doesn't half improve a plain lamb. Put it like this explained my local farmer: "Claudia Schiffer can roll out of bed, rub the sleep out of her eyes and look stunning but my Missus isn't really fit to be seen out without a bit of makeup on."

Now I know who he is, he knows who he is, but his wife doesn't and I know she reads this page so he had better be pleasant to me for a week or two.

Mind over matter

WHEN I was a kid at school, I always liked the German concentration camp jokes. My favourite is when the camp commandant stood in front of the inmates and announced: "Today, we prove mind over matter - that we don't mind and you don't matter." Sounds a bit like present day dealings with the Ministry of Agriculture. There's also a similarity in dressing up some thing as good news when it's no such thing (e.g. £500 million which doesn't put an extra pound in your pocket). Today a change of underwear, Hut A will change with Hut B, B will change with C...

Can-r-Cum

I was at the Westmorland County Show and was quite surprised when I got to the NFU tent. There was an eight foot high board showing Ben Gill, and what was next to it - another eight foot board with a picture of Can-R-Cum at the Blackpool rally last back-end. It's a bit unnerving keeping catching an eight foot picture of your daughter out of the corner of your eye.

Dual controls

I was amused talking to a member whose neighbour was a good hand at making the air turn blue across the valley when running his dog. He went on to explain he also could easily tell when he had visitors in their caravans as the dog had then to contend with instructions in the Queen's English - and I think it still did as it liked.

County Chairman

I was fortunate enough to be invited to the NFU AGM in the year 2000 and spent some time in the company of that year's Cumbria County Chairman, Harold Armstrong. We shared a few sherberts and took great pleasure in poking fun at each other, which continued into the year's NFU magazine, as follows.

Harold: In reply to Mike's Mumblings or Sanderson's Ramblings of last month where he referred to solving his tax problems by taking a farm, perhaps I could solve mine by becoming a group secretary, and then I might have some to pay.

Mike: I was pleased to see in last month's magazine the County Chairman reads this rubbish and fancies being a group secretary. My wife suggested I give him a swap - he might manage the IACS forms but I think a Wigton dairy farmer would get altitude sickness lambing yows on Shap.

I'm not sure if our County Chairman, Harold Armstrong, will include his favourite moment in his notes - standing having a piddle only to be joined by Franz Fischler.

Harold: My contacts in Appleby have informed me of a sign spotted in Swaggering Sanderson's office. It reads: "Simple questions answered - £5; more difficult questions answered - £10; dumb looks are still free." (Mike's speciality). Needless to say the kitty is empty.

Mike: I reported last month that I had had a medical problem. I understand our illustrious County Chairman has also had his problems. The word is he's been to his doctor to have his sex drive lowered. His doctor examined him and explained as with most men his age it was all in his mind. Poor Harold had to explain that's why he wanted it lowering.

The last time I saw my mate the illustrious County Chairman, he had a smug look and a sly grin on his face, so goodness only knows what he's going to come up with in the next edition in the form of revenge, but don't believe a word, it's all lies - honest!

Harold: Following the publication of last month's journal, I was stopped on the road by a neighbour who asked me if the picture of Sanderson was an old one, to which I replied: "That's what he looks like now." My neighbour had thought he was a lot older going by the age of the jokes he tells and I have to say that I found it difficult to disagree with him.

Mike: Did you notice last month I was squeezed into a corner? It wasn't lack of inspiration on my part but the sharpness of the editor's knife. (I didn't realise the County Chairman had that much influence.) The

NOT S'MANY COWS AND A LOT LESS YOWS

piece they cut just shows the type of summer we're having. It was written when the first cut men were tearing their hair out trying to silage and should have been read on the hottest week of the year when everyone was hay timing. Goodness only knows what the weather will be doing when you're reading this now - no doubt a deluge or a drought.

My column was moved back with the rest of my colleagues in Cumbria (not that there's anything wrong with that, of course). I've lost my own page and you don't have to look at my ugly mug any more. The moral of the story is - don't cross the County Chairman.

Harold: We have just held the county elections meeting and I can't believe it is a year since the last one. My congratulations go to Stephen Dunning who became County Vice Chairman. I hope that he gets as much enjoyment out of his three years as I have. On the same night we had Old Mike from Appleby signing his new books "Ewes and Moos" so it was very difficult to get in for the queue, which extended to almost three people at one point. I have actually acquired a copy, which is signed by his own fair hand. I thought that I might keep it as I saw a first edition of the Harry Potter book sold recently for quite a large amount of money.

The final word

Harold was good enough to pen a few lines as a review for my book *Yows and Cows* and finished his year as County Chairman with this poem:

My year as County Chairman
Has been a lot of fun
The only fly in the ointment
Has been Mike Sanderson

He's used me and abused me
He's made me truly age
He convinced some Journal readers
That I lost him his page

And stand back Jeffrey Archer
For Mike has gone to press
With Yows and Cows, the novel
A runaway success

I hate to burst the bubble
But I have to break the news
That people are just buying it
To read the book reviews.

Harold Armstrong.

Two for the price of three

MUCH to the amusement of Mr Pigney, I was followed on to his fore-court and given a severe lecture by a police officer for not wearing my seat belt in the week prior to Gypsy week. He thought it would have read wonderfully well in the local press if the local NFU man had been done. He also asked me to remind you of Pigney's special summer sale. Two for the price of Three and, yes, I have got it the right way round.

Overdraft worries

I was tickled by the story of the farmer who was having a consultation with his bank manager. The bank manager explained he was very worried about the farm overdraft - the farmer said that was grand and he wasn't too bothered as it was pointless two of them worrying about it.

11th June

THE 11 June was a bit of a red letter day at Kirkby Stephen - the first Tuesday night lamb sale. It was a bit low key and there wasn't a lot of stock about and the main talking point was the 'bio-security rules'. I would agree it seems over the top - we've either got foot and mouth or we haven't. I liked the notice on the 'Gents' door - you had to check your bio-security on entry, on exit... and during.

Willcock

I was poking fun at our County Chairman last month wearing Wendy Harrison's identity badge. Well he's been having more trouble with badges. I am reliably informed he attended a meeting at the Kendal Show ground and his badge rechristened him "Willcock Bain". I have come across one or two acquaintances who could have earned a christian name like that but surely not our Will!!

Pardon

Son, James, is thirteen now so I thought it was about time he got put on a tractor. You never know when you'll need a haybob operator. I set him off chain harrowing on my old (1968) David Brown and he managed quite well. I thought he'd be thrilled, but no, he just complained the old girl made his ears hurt! I explained: "That, son, is why I am always saying pardon."

A waiting game

I was travelling home one evening back to Appleby out of Maulds Meaburn up on to Meaburn Edge when I was flagged down by a young man waiting to turn stock into a field. We had the crack and he explained his father was fetching some stirks out of a field further up the road. We waited and waited, so I said I would turn them into the field if he wanted to go and give the old man a hand. I waited and waited and waited and waited and three quarters of an hour later nothing had happened. I didn't dare leave the scene just in case these stirks did appear but apparently they preferred running round the field to being moved to fresh grazing.

Politically correct

WE'VE been clipping and were busy marking our Cheviots and we had a couple of wooled Swaledale strays in with them. They were a bit uneasy and a bit wild (you could even say they were a bit sheepish). Son, James, had the answer: "What do you expect, they're an ethnic minority."

We'd been gathering the fell beside the M6 and he'd picked up a few cats eyes that had been thrown over the fence. When we got back to the farm James was arranging them on the concrete path to the back door. Granda asked what he thought he was doing, so he explained it was so he could find his way into the house when he came home from the pub. Granda just said: "Huh" and disappeared into the house. James then thought he probably didn't need them as he had managed for the last forty odd years!

Over-grazing

WITH Tony going with over half our sheep last year and only doing "natural" restocking, we've more than enough grass. One allotment in particular, was well mucked in winter and only had the tups and a few wether hoggs and they were taken off over a month ago! There's that much grass you can hardly see the thistles! I was leading some yows and lambs to it after clipping and told the old man if he couldn't see them I hadn't put them in the wrong field, it was just the grass. When I asked a day or two after if he'd seen them he said: "just bits of their backs."

NFU popularity

YOU will be delighted to know some farmers are extremely pleased to see their local NFU man. One in particular I am thinking about was busy gardening under duress. He took me inside for a cup of tea and said the job we had to do would just last long enough so it would be time for him to go and get his cows when we finished.

A mole?

MY mate, the County Chairman, appears to have found a mole in the Appleby area spying on me on Pigney's forecourt. It doesn't take a genius to work out, does it Fireman Mole

Well, I've got my own sources. I know Will likes big bikes and like a lot of others relives his youth on Sunday afternoons and puts the rest of us motorists at risk. He would take his wife on a romantic jaunt on a beautiful summer's evening. Unfortunately, the bike broke down and the poor lass ended up pushing Will and the bike in a fruitless attempt to start it. She eventually ended up being worried with midges and being led home in the back of the cattle trailer. You know how to treat the girls, Will!

Hause Farm

A few know and for anyone who's interested, the old man is retiring and we will be giving up the farm in February next year - Mam's that poorly he really has no choice. I wouldn't have minded 'a go', but the landlord deemed it was not to be. A lot of the problems with farms to sell or let now, is the value is all in the farmhouse and the land is just a by-product - you could call it asset stripping.

All tied up

WE got our hay/crop tied up but not without the help of the big baler. Mike from Terry's Farm came to our rescue and did a good job. He was on our steepest most awkward field and not one bale got off on him. I learned afterwards he was being extra careful so he didn't appear in these pages, so I didn't want to disappoint him! I was going to warn him to look out for rabbit-holes when he pulled into the field, but as every wheel on his outfit was about three foot wide, he didn't have to bother. It's a bit different to our tackle.

Jonathan Dixon's bats

DID you hear they'd had a barbecue at Nateby and the lights had attracted some bats and they got in the house? No - I didn't think it was very interesting either but I did like the headline.

Rather more amusing, was a scrape he'd had and we received a letter quoting the accident date in 1900. I commented I hadn't realised his old truck was that old, he said he didn't realise he was that old.

A good show

CAN-R-CUM was determined to show something at Appleby Show and borrowed Mother's dog for the lurcher class. It hadn't been off the farm since it was a pup and barked all night. Well, it barked until 3am when I got up with the damned thing and slept downstairs with it. Mr. Pigney got wind of it and it amused him no end and he was spreading rumours I was sleeping with the dog instead of my wife! Can-R-Cum got two second places with him (Fred) but the highlight of his afternoon was piddling on Piggie's stand's floral display.

Deputy County Chairman

I have had a dig at the County Chairman, but his deputy, Steve Dunning, has been causing us a bit of fun. He's broken the middle finger of his left hand and he's left handed. He assures us he was kicked by a cow, but local gossip is rife. There's all sorts of suggestions, even a chastity belt. Steve says not to worry - he's ambidextrous and can drink with both hands.

22 September 2002

YOU should have this magazine before the 22nd, so finally, if you're wondering whether to go or not - GO. The last march with over a quarter of a million in London shook Tony in his boots. Think what a million will do.

Uncle Bryan's first fax
UNCLE has finally moved into the 21st century and purchased a fax machine. Earlier, I had fallen heir to a picture of him Cumbria Police had

rejected for his gun licence, so I blew it up and produced his first fax (see picture). There are a good many reasons why they could have rejected it (looking like a criminal) but the reason was, he was wearing a hat.

M6 banner

IF you've travelled north up the M6, I hope you've seen the "Keep Britain Milking" signs we have put up in father's top field on Shap Summit. It was a pretty windy day when we did it and you soon realise how sailing ships work and where the next wind farm should be sited. A wind farm and a perfect poster site - we've just realised too late we were sitting on a fortune.

It'll come in

THE beacon on Orton Scar for the build up to the Countryside March was quite a useful tool when you're clearing up for a farm sale. And before it even starts to cross your mind, there was no black plastic or tyres involved - honest. There were old doors, pallets and gates to be replaced. I was loading up an old gate that had been there as long as I can remember and father insisted I took the old chain and hook off it before tipping it as it "would come in!" I guess in the next month or two we'll be coming across things that have been going to come in for the last 47 years.

Look out for a breeding sheep sale at Kirkby and a vintage machinery sale on 2 November.

Dropped in it

I'D been at Buckles Farm and had finished my business and was turning the car round to come away. I can't have been paying enough attention to my job as I dropped the front wheel of the car in a dug out drain and could neither go backwards or forwards. I went to my host for assistance and with the car leaning over at a jaunty angle, he thought he'd rather look for a camera than a tow rope and send the picture to this publication. Fortunately, I do carry a tow rope and got pulled out before a camera appeared and avoided further embarrassment.

Dunning's detours

WE marched with the 400,000 and what a day out. I went down by car with Steve Dunning and my kids. The plan was to hit the end of the M1 and find a tube station, we got "semi-lost" but saw Wembley. I knew for certain there was a station there, so that's where we went, but Steve's map reading had amused the kids.

They slept most of the way back - James woke up to see a sign for Newcastle (Under Lyme) and thought he was in the North East and laughed, thinking Steve's map reading had gone awry again. We marched past St James Park and James asked: "This isn't the real St James Park is it?" I assured him the real one was in the North East where a REAL centre-forward played.

Civilised Dipping

THIS back-end at Hause Farm saw us in a bit of a quandary, we had always dipped our sheep at this time of year to prevent sheep scab and lice, but this year the Government in their wisdom had taken organsphosphorous dips off the market and the alternatives we are led to believe although kinder to humans aren't all that brilliant for sheep. Non-farmers might wonder why our great leaders took the most effective treatment for sheep scab off the market.

Well OP dips aren't too kind to humans and some farmers suffer terribly with OP poisoning, in some parts it's known as sheep dip flue and the symptoms are pretty similar to flu, it can also affect the nervous system and OPs are actually used in making "nerve gas". So our great leaders were worried about the farmer's health? NO. They are worried they might have some claims up their backs as they've been making farmers compulsorily dip with it for donkeys years, so they banned it because the containers are not safe, not the dip itself. So no come back on them then!

All this didn't help our dilemma over what to do with our yows so we took the modern way out and injected them instead of dipping them and put them in the hands of modern science. All had gone well until nicely into the new year when some of them started to itch and scratch. By now OP dip had got a temporary licence but we were again in a quandary, our sheep were half way to lambing and our dipping tub was built 45 years ago for Rough Fell yows which are a bit smaller than in lamb Cheviots.

Would we have to turn to modern technology again and use a sheep shower? Well we did but I'd never seen one working before, it's a round metal pen ten feet or so high, you drive a dozen or so sheep in and they get squirted with dip from above and below, are left for a minute to drain and they're finished with. I have to admit our old girls hadn't seen one before so they ran in relatively easily, they might not another time but it bears no resemblance to traditional dipping.

There's no battle to pen them as they never forget the dipper and catching pen. There's no dragging them every inch across a half acre catching pen and gently persuading them to reverse in to the tub, there's no turning them and pushing their heads under while they have their feet wedged on one side of the tub and their backs on the other, there's no eyeful of dip as one goes in easier than expected and you get drenched. In fact there's almost no sweating at all; on a cold day the biggest problem could be keeping warm.

I'm not too sure what the poor old yows thought though. They must have got the shock of their lives when they got squirted at pressure from above and below. I tell you what it isn't half wet in there, it wouldn't be long of soaking you to the skin, that of course is the whole idea. No I don't think they'd reckon much to it, getting dipped without the pleasure of making you sweat, swear and in my case blister my hands on the posher, not half as much fun as proper dipping - far too civilised.

Some style

I have got to mention Nick Utting at Carlisle who, if you've not heard has broken his leg. I've had so many folk ring me to make sure I know, I don't want to disappoint them. Apparently, he fell with some style - or in reality in stile whilst walking - he really should take more water with it! I understand he's hopping mad!

Keep them right

ONE serious point - I am getting an increasing number of enquiries regarding cattle records being cocked up at Workington as they now can mess up your Beef, Suckler and Slaughter claims. You shouldn't have to, but I strongly recommend you check their records are correct or you could lose a lot of money - Not only have you to keep your own records straight, but their's as well!

Smiling

ONE young farmer walked into the office at Kirkby after having a hell of a trade, he was grinning from ear to ear. I had to inform him smiling was not the done thing, but he promised me he had not grinned in the ring - honest. If he or anyone else needs tuition I know a soon to be retired farmer who is the county's expert at looking as miserable as sin whilst having a flying trade.

Holidays

Standing in the mart office while they were issuing licences for bought tups, the vast majority were off on their holidays. They weren't going to where they had been bought but off on their holidays to a holding until they could be taken home when sales, etc. and the 21 day standstill allow. It's perfectly legal, but causing hundreds of extra movements which is just what our friends in high places are trying to avoid but are forcing working folk into - ignorant or what!

Hectic

OCTOBER has been a hectic month getting ready for father's farm sale, along with all the tup sales. We'll be virtually out of sheep now but we have kept the kids' yows and they have gone to Uncle Bryan's. Can-R-Cum took a picture of them so you can see Tessa, Floppy and Pop-Eye (it's the luckiest sheep in Cumbria - it jumped in off the fell the day before they were culled). It's not a speck on the camera, it's a black spot in the middle of its forehead - see the photograph on page 60.

They've gone to see Uncle Bryan's Billie Beltex. He's a funny look-ing thing with little short legs (the tup that is!). He doesn't look fast enough to catch our Cheviot crosses (or mongrels as Uncle called then) never mind do any good once he does catch up with them. Time will no doubt tell.

In charge

I came back from Hawes Auction and informed Tina they had a notice on the office wall which read: "Do you want to talk to the man in charge, or the woman who knows what's going on." Tina thought she wanted one - so did Janet Bell at Kirkby Stephen Auction when I told her about it.

Leicesters

JOHN Cloughton was selling Leicesters at Hawes and it was getting late on. Uncle Bryan was in attendance but was not paying a lot of attention when John clattered the rostrum: "Three thousand one hundred pounds - Bryan Cousin." I think poor old uncle nearly had a pink fit, much to the amusement of the whole auction. He did a bit of spluttering but it had been a Welshman behind him who'd been bidding.

I was being berated at the insurance rates for Leicester tups but was defending myself because of their ability to point all four legs skyward and I was informed: "Leicesters don't die often you know - only once!".

I was there
I was stood watching when the first £100,000 Swaledale tup was sold, the atmosphere was electric, you could hear a pin drop. The auctioneer, Maurice Scott was brilliant and milked it for all it was worth at £100,000 he was looking around the auction asking: "Are you looking at me?" I certainly wasn't, I wouldn't have dared twitch.

Computer Virus
THE atmosphere was a bit like Alan Shearer scoring the winner in the fifth minute of injury time in the Cup Final against Man. Utd. Speaking of Manchester United, have you heard they've named a computer virus after them. It makes your computer think it's much better than it really is but it has a memory disorder and it can't recall anything before 1993.

There's also a Roy Keane virus that's particularly nasty and keeps throwing you out of windows, then there's the Fabien Barthez virus which isn't really harmful, it just won't save anything.

Farm Sale
THERE seems to have been an awful lot of water passed under the bridge since I sat down to write last month's notes. We've had our farm sale we're out of cattle and have sold almost all the sheep.

None of it's been easy but the hardest day was selling the breeding sheep at Kirkby. The kids were there and there were a few tears shed and no doubt there'll be a few more before we're finished.

Farm sales are a wonderful institution people come and pay YOU money to take YOUR rubbish away. We were marvellously supported by family, friends and neighbours alike and I must say a big thank you to them. We didn't make a fortune but we didn't have anything that was worth a fortune. Brian Hogg from Murton, an expert in such things explained before the sale not to take any notice of what things made, as some would be a lot less than you thought and others would be more. He was dead right although he wasn't right when he bet the auctioneer he wouldn't buy anything - he couldn't resist the temptation.

I think the cheapest item was a box of haybob tynes I hadn't got round to smashing and the dearest could have been my old tractor - way over cost price. I spoke to the lad who bought it and he told me he was on a mission. His old scraper tractor had given up the ghost and if he didn't get the tractor bought it would have to be a shovel and it wasn't going to be the shovel.

It did seem to be that any of the tackle to do with handling little bales that were very cheap. Nobody seems to want to lead bales or be able to find anyone who'll lead bales for them. Father never seemed to have a problem. Pay a decent rate, pay up on time, feed them well and knock off at least an hour before the pub shuts. I think another attraction was they could come and give the old man as much abuse as they liked without fear of any reprisals - bale leading is one job you DON'T get the sack from.

The Old Baler

FATHER'S old baler was an absolute snip. It would be 30 years old but almost exclusively used by father himself. It was very rarely I was allowed anywhere near it. He always set the tractor at exactly the right revs and never altered it and always selected a suitably low gear. He was a good hand at timing it so the last bale was made as either the bale leaders or the bale stackers caught up. And if they hadn't the baler was always to clean off. I think it was the only implement that was always put inside for winter - it was his pride and joy. It was just about the first thing he bought brand new. He always says if it missed a bale it wasn't the baler's fault and it generally was something else like bad string. See the photograph on page 62.

Twisted Leg

THE week after the farm sale I was getting down off the hay mew (there was no ladder - it had been sold!) and really badly turned my ankle. I soldiered on that day but it blew up like a balloon and I had to give in next day and go to casualty. Initially they reckoned it was broken which was a blow. My first reaction was what a damned nuisance and very quickly the second was how much stick will I get off Nick Utting at Carlisle after I'd taken great pleasure out of taking the rise out of him. To his credit he was very sympathetic, I must admit in his position I doubt I wouldn't have been.

Anyone who grumbles about the cost of their insurance wants to have a look in casualty and see the heap of leaflets for ambulance chasing "no win no fee" solicitors. There was even an advert on the back of my appointment card. It crossed my mind I might sue the old hill farmer who sold the ladder but I soon thought better of it. The broken leg turned out to be better than expected and ended up in a splint and not a plaster. I could get my boots on once I'd taken my knife to the elastic sides and could get in about a size nine and size eleven wellie. I did get a bit of stick in the auction when I got accused of being tight and wearing up odd wellies.

Shortly after being laid up with my twisted ankle, I received the following anonymous letter which has my mate Harold Armstrong's finger prints all over it. He's never owned up to it though.

Hop   **HAGS**
Along
Group
Secretaries

Dear Sir,

I am writing to you to see if you would be interested in joining the above group. This is a very selective close-knit club whose founder member is of course none other than Sir N Utting MBE.

Perhaps I could spell out some of the benefits of membership of this exclusive club. First of all it goes without saying that it entitles you to free use of all medical aids to make getting around easier. These include not only such things as crutches, walking sticks, plasters and leg callipers but motorised wheelchairs and quad bikes are also available. The inclusion of quad bikes would be of particular interest to you when you are trying to corner a farmer who stubbornly is always across a ploughed field when you call.

As this is a non-profit making society we have managed to keep the membership fee to a very reasonable £250 per annum or 50p per acre, whichever is the greater. Any surplus monies are of course remitted to the honourable society retired County Chairman which I am sure you will agree is a very good and deserving cause. Looking forward to a favourable and early reply.

Yours sincerely,   Mr. B R O Kenleg Sec

And the reply:

Peasant Farmers Union
Upt Valley
Westmorland

Dear Sir,

re HAGS
(Harold Armstrong's Gay Society)

Many thanks for your recent communication with regard to the above club, but I feel I am no longer in a position to contribute to your funds. Not only do I no longer limp I do not have a limp wrist.

I do understand you also run a most worthwhile charity of which you are the founder member, the fund For Underachieving Chairman Kicked Out For Fun. If you were to send details of the above I would be happy to subscribe.

Yours sincerely,
Mr X Hopper

Sweepings Up

THE only sheep we have left to sell will soon go and are the last of the wether lambs, the "sweepings up" you might call them; not the sort you can stand in the ring with and puff your chest out with pride! Father tells a nice tale of being in the ring at Kendal with a similar collection and being asked by the auctioneer if he could say something about them. After much thought, the best he could come up with was: "Well they've lived this long!"

A swinging time

IT'S strange now being on the farm at present. For one thing all the stock has gone and it's a bit like a ghost town but just as strange are the gates - they swing. As with most retiring tenant farmers, there's been a bit of maintenance work to catch up with. After watching gates swing that I have carried round for as long as I can remember, it's just a pity this work didn't get done ten years ago and we'd have got a bit of benefit out of it ourselves.

Hop along

I wrote last month about my bad ankle and I guess if I'd have done as I was told and been signed off work for four weeks it would have been better by now. Being hill farmer bred, I'm not very good at doing as I am told and have tried my best to soldier on. It aches a bit of a night and I could do with a kick-start in a morning, but I can manage. My mate, Mr Pigney laughingly advises me if I was four stone lighter, it would heal quicker - well he would know wouldn't he!

Another virus

A while ago, I was poking fun at Manchester United and their computer viruses AND which weekend did this damned magazine come out - the weekend Newcastle lost 5-3 at Old Trafford - I can take a bit of stick and it's just as well.

There's a David Beckham virus as well you know - looks lovely, all the lights are on but there's nothing going on inside! Still on the football theme I was poking fun at Gill Shearer our 'PR' lady at Skelmersdale and local editor of the NFU magazine - did she know they sang a song about her at St James Park: "Same old Shearer. Always scoring!"

Cattle on the internet

FATHER'S cattle have gone and I think the paperwork was a bigger fight then the cattle, even though they hadn't been handled for at least 18 months (that could easily apply to the paperwork as well!) What did help was being able to look on the internet and see what the BCMS at Workington thought you had.

They're anything but foolproof though. I have come across someone who, according to them, had no cattle in January 2002, which was correct, and three months later in April he had heaps of cattle which was also correct but included in them were a collection of FMD culled animals. It would be interesting to know where Workington thought these FMD cattle were in January - had they just flown in from heaven?

Don't laugh too much, if you don't realise the mistakes they've made, they're all your fault.

Diversification

I'M not at all keen on do it yourself and if the wife's ever got after me my excuse has always been father has an urgent job at Hause Farm. With father down to two dogs and a cat, I was reduced to assembling "flat pack" bunk beds. Father had taken a look at the bits and decided they were just a heap of kindling. Quite surprisingly for me I almost completed it but realised there were some holes in some bits of wood where they shouldn't have been. Fortunately, my brother in law 'our Brian' who's much handier than me, soon put some holes in and sorted it out - it's MUCH, MUCH easier dealing with crazy Cheviot yows you know.

Rabbits
TO finish, what do you call a Saudi who has a belt with half a dozen rabbits tied on to it Bin Lamping.

A look back at 2002 from up the valley, written for the Cumberland & Westmorland Herald, Christmas 2002
TWELVE months ago looking forward to 2002, I would have liked to have seen things in the farming world getting back to what we would think of as normal after the foot and mouth debacle. Twelve months later, it is becoming increasingly obvious nothing of the sort is going to happen.

The first thing everyone wanted to see disappear was the bureaucracy involved with anything to do with moving livestock. Although some of the licensing has eventually slipped away, we are still left with this ludicrous 20 day rule stopping everything moving off a farm for three weeks once an animal has moved on. It makes no sense whatsoever and makes farming livestock in the area nigh on impossible. It has been quite legitimately and legally got around, by moving stock on and off different holdings to suit the paperwork. It makes for extra unnecessary movements. It also encourages illegal movements all of which are exactly what is not wanted, but there are no boffins, vets or politicians brave enough in London to get out of their ivory towers and come down on the side of common sense. Surely a sensible less onerous system would deliver more of what all sides want.

In the Upper Eden Valley, 2002 has seen a dramatic relocation of the area's dairy herd, numerous medical sized milk herds have not been replaced because of downward pressure on the milk price and the economies of scale see all the bigger herds keeping another 50 or 100 cows. You can see where it is heading and I suppose it's progress, but I'm not sure it's for the best.

You can't look back in 2002 in these parts without mention of our auction companies. We've seen Penrith, Farmers' and Kidd's give up the ghost on livestock auctioning with others more than willing to jump in and take their place. We have seen so many of the figures in the public domain, but it strikes me there's more to it than meets the eye! Time will no doubt tell.

Crackers or not so crackers

NEITHER can you look back at 2002 in these parts and not talk about the record breaking £100,000 Swaledale tup. I wasn't called on but I am quite sure I could have justified it to the press or TV. I didn't study economics at school but I understand supply and demand, a large percentage of the Swaledale flock were slaughtered and people were quite rightly compensated to replace them. It stands to reason, with only a certain number of quality tups the price was going to reflect the situation.

One hundred thousand pounds is an awful lot of money for one animal, but if you reckon he could quite easily get twenty tup lambs at £5000 you're soon into profit, and if he can manage one or two more then away you go.

The actual sale of the tup himself was pure theatre. The ring was jam packed because he was that day's first prize winner. Maurice Scott was in the box auctioning him and milked the occasion brilliantly and you could hear a pin drop. As the price went up and up, he waved the hammer around the ring asking: "Are you looking at me? Are there any more bids as there are a lot more to sell."

"Tek your time, tek your time," demanded the vendor, a certain Mr Slack of Stoneriggs. Absolute magic it was. Mr Scott was walking on air for weeks to come. It certainly wasn't the best of PR for hill farming, but it certainly shut up the snipers over valuations of pedigree stock. It didn't do the tup insurance man any harm either!

Advice

ONE of the more interesting things this year, has been watching folk go back after foot and mouth. Some have jumped right back in, others have just dipped their toes in the water. I've been asked many times for my opinion and all I can say is they'll have to ask someone a bit wiser than me. There is one thing on the increase, and that's organisations and bodies dishing out advice but I'm not sure they're any wiser than me either. Go with your gut feeling and do what suits you and your farm set-up the best - and certainly not what attracts most grant.

Personally

FROM a personal point of view, 2002 has been just as traumatic as foot and mouth in 2001. Because of illness we've had to give up Hause Farm and sell up. Stock dispersal sales and farm sales were every bit as hard as FMD culls. Although I have not lived at Hause Farm all my life, it's always been part of my life and it's just disappeared in front of my eyes. Friends, neighbours and family were all very supportive but it's still hard when everything you've worked with for years disappears out of the farm gate. And finally - 2002 in a nut shell: Change at an ever increasing rate on the road to...

Approaching fifty

TIME keeps rolling on. I'm now in my 14th year at Appleby and nearer 50 than 40. It's starting to show as well, both Tina and I in recent weeks have made appointments then just clean forgotten about them (senior moments I think some people call them). So if you tell me something - MAKE SURE I write it down!

Correct?

IT'S not just my mind - as well as suffering with a bad ankle, I've also been bothered with an abscess on a tooth. I'm no lover of dentists and think they often like to cure your problems by spending as much of your money as they can. Well, I insisted on a simple extraction and got one and it's the best £43 I've spent for a long time. With a badly swollen face my children were very sympathetic: "Dad, you look like a frog."

It's the first tooth I have lost as an adult and, as was pointed out to me by a lady group secretary at Carlisle, I am no longer "correct" of the mouth   But still correct below.

Bio-security

I was told a nice one about a local farmer harassing the trading standard's man about not doing his job properly. Did he not know there was someone about who was working both nationally and internationally and didn't bother about trading standards, bio-security or licences? He said if there was a reward he would make him wiser. Unfortunately, there was no reward, but after much questioning the farmer finally let slip the identity of the miscreant - Father Christmas.

The same man asked me if I know the only qualifications needed by a land agent - their father and mother have not got to be joined in holy wedlock! I think I can vouch for that one!

The last load!

WE'VE finally got Mam and Dad moved down to Shap. Bob, who usually helps us among the sheep gave us a hand with the furniture and I told him the last load would be the hardest, rounding up the old man and chasing him in the trailer. The women folk had the answer, once his old chair was burnt, his bed had gone and he hadn't a cup to make a coffee, the poor old bugger had no choice but to follow on.

Just about the hardest part has been the sheep dogs. Mr Rap is fully retired and is going to live in the village once his deluxe dog kennel is completed, but Glen has gone up Wet Sleddale to Henry Harrison. There was no charge but a couple of stipulations. He must look after him well and Can-R-Cum has had to have full visiting rights.

To remember it all by, we've had Kevin Alderson do us a picture of the dogs which is reproduced on page 59. He really is a gifted lad and knowing his father, I've no idea where he gets it from.

Icy

THE morning of Thursday, 9 January - do you remember it? An inch of ice everywhere. I didn't even dare set off with the car and was making my way very gingerly down our street which is very steep. Mike Sowerby from Terry's Farm who lives at the bottom of the street didn't dare set off to Ormside either and was stood in his front door. As I slid past, he produced his camera and said he was waiting for me to fall then take my picture. More by good luck then good management, I didn't oblige him - rotten beggar.

Stop press

OUR last three sheep belonging to my kids have all been scanned with twins. Uncle Bryan's in charge and pointed out they shouldn't count their chickens. I think Can-R-Cum after trailing about on a hill farm during lambing time for a dozen years or more with her Granda is fully aware of this.

Still time

WE'VE got until 10 March to put our thoughts in about this 'Right to Roam' so there's still time. On studying the map, I see they have Warcop Range designated - that's the spot for all these ramblers. I am sure the NFU could see their way to supplying fluorescent T-shirts with targets on them!

Finally

THERE was a beautiful sunrise, one of those really frosty mornings and I said to son, James, come and look at this: "Red sky in the morning,"

"But Dad," he said, "we're not shepherds anymore..."

RU04FUN

THERE'S getting to be quite a few of these folk who're into personalised registration numbers in NFU circles. There's been J111NFU about for a bit and I see her mate at Penrith's got one now, A15NFU or something similar - poseur. There's a couple of them floating about at Carlisle as well and even an NFU man at Kendal who keeps changing his Volvo and hanging on to his old "L" registration number. I think he thinks we're all that daft we won't notice.

I took the mick out of H3TUP a bit since and thought it might have been H3WETHER but I've come across my first tractor with a person-alised number M002JRS - I think. I thought M002COW would have been better but the young man said it was too dear. After the young farmers performance at their Valentine's do in Appleby when their routine ended up with them in their flat caps, wellies and thongs perhaps STR1P would be more appropriate - or even 1NCH.

Good luck to them though, they raised a lot of money and had a good night.

NFU Delhi branch

! was speaking to a lady from the Norwich Union just a day or two after it had been announced their call centres were going to be moved to India. She was a right helpful lass and after a bit I asked her if she was from Bangladesh. "No, she wasn't she was from bloody Preston," and wasn't too pleased about their jobs being exported.

As far as I am aware, the NFU have no plans to move any of us to India, although I can think of some who sit in their ivory towers down in

London and Stratford upon Avon who could do with being moved a bit further away!

Hard or what

I had reason to be in the sheep pens at Bleathgill on Stainmore where they were jabbing yows with Dectomax. It was one of those bitterly cold frosty days and it's a bit exposed up there, although not quite as bad as Shap! I was admiring his toughness when he opened his jacket to reveal a hot water bottle tied around his neck. He swore blind it was to stop the Dectomax freezing. I wasn't too sure.

DAFTA

THEY really do drive you daft. At the beginning of February they sent out hundreds and thousands of letters telling hill farmers they weren't hard enough stocked to receive their Hill Farm Allowance and put the fear of god up folk, and then admitted a day or two later they shouldn't have been sent out at all. This causing panic in the countryside and the poor NFU man numerous telephone calls all for no reason. It was easier just pressing a button than stopping and thinking.

Then what happens, ten years after they made everyone spend a fortune on maps, they produce them for everyone for nowt. If you haven't got your new digital maps yet, they're very accurate and up to date. They'll just about show if you have left a bucket in the middle of a field.

Auction Mart fun

YOU can get a giggle on a Tuesday night in the auction at Kirkby Stephen. Young, Ted Ogden had just finished selling lambs and there was a pause before they moved on to old yows and tups. There was a large Cheviot tup in the ring when Ted returned to business.

"That's a tremendous yow - who'll bid me £25." Much to everyone's amusement it was pointed out to him it was a tup. Did it knock him back - not likely. He just laughed and said: "The moral to this is Don't go out with me on a Saturday night."

As if that wasn't enough, it wasn't long after when an old billy goat with horns about two foot long came into the ring and cleared it of dealers in about ten seconds flat. They were either fleeing over the rails or standing on their tip toes on the benches.

Life in the old dog yet

OUR old dog was about retired before we'd finished on the farm. He still liked to do a bit but strictly on his terms. We don't know if he's taking to retirement in the bungalow too well. Father quite happily turned him into the garden which has a decent stone wall round it, secure in the knowledge he couldn't get out. Can-R-Cum got him a dog tag for Xmas and it's just as well. Father got a phone call: "Have you got a dog called Rap?"

"Yes, he's in the garden."

"No he isn't, he's in the old folks home."

The old beggar had jumped out and gone for a wander. The old man's having to put a jumping wire up to keep his dog in.

Mr Rap

I'VE written many many times about our old dog and he's even held in such esteem in the family, he's usually called Mister Rap. The kid and I often amuse ourselves by making rhymes about him. Here it is strung together:

Think of the miles he's run for us
Think of the fells he's trod
Think of all the work he's done
That little black and white dog.

He's got no bits of paper
No fancy pedigree
To graft all day and never give in
That's his guarantee.

He'd never win a sheepdog trial
He is no Fancy Dan
For effort and a job well done
Mister Rap's yer man.

There's lots and lots of clever dogs
But none like Mister Rap
When he's got no sheep to work
He goes and walls a gap.

Mr Rap he is no saint
He has his little quirks
Like piddling on the tablecloth
And eating afterbirth.

Mr Rap thinks he knows best
He thinks he's always right
They say dogs grow like their owners
And now you know its right   (sorry Dad!)

Mr Rap is growing old
His muzzle's growing grey
To have him five years old again
What we wouldn't pay.

Mr Rap's a hero
Mr Rap's a star
Mr Rap does everything
He even drives the car.

Think of the miles he's run for us
Think of the fells he's trod
Think of all those happy years
That marvellous little dog.

I realise he's no better and no worse than the vast majority of collie dogs. The only difference is he's OUR collie dog.

Reg. numbers
LAST month I poked fun at a few of my colleagues but missed the best one, Chris Davies at Kendal whose jeep is something like J33CJD. No one's sure if it is to do with his initials or his state of mind.

County executive meeting
CALLING all NFU members. It's safe to go to these meetings again and get home the same day. We don't put up with too much "bull manure" in this corner of the country and our local chairman got the last meeting finished by 9 o'clock - well done, Steve.

Fast (geld) lady
WE had the pleasure of our new Policy Advisor's presence at our last branch meeting and I think she had an interesting evening. She was going to travel over Orton Scar with the County Chairman, but he was otherwise engaged so his son gave her lift. I think the trip was more than quick. She arrived looking very pale!

During the meeting, she was very informative until it got to understanding local farming terms - she wasn't sure what a geld cow was. I put her straight and told her I hoped she WAS geld. I didn't think I'd be able to make her blush! I'm not sure how her evening ended but Steve Dunning was taking her back and assured her he was quicker than his son! (What do you reckon?)

Easy peasy lambing
LAMBING time's a doddle this year. As I've said Uncle Bryan's got the kids' yows and they're all scanned with twins to "Billy Beltex". Well, two of them have safely produced their lambs and all it's consisted of is picking up a text message on the mobile from Cousin Ian. We have been to see they're OK and to take a picture or two (see page ...)

Writing this towards the end of March, it's been a super time for lambing, cold nights but lovely days. I was asking a hill man if he'd got a start to lamb: "No, my old yows are waiting for the bad weather."

CAP reform

THIS is the subject that is causing me the most enquiries at present and it is extremely difficult to really help. I can only tell folk what we think, they think they think they're going to do. You could be better looking in your crystal ball or asking your fairy godmother. It beats me how anyone's supposed to make any sensible business decisions - they might even end up doing nowt.

The next most popular topic is disposal of dead sheep. How the powers that be can introduce these rules when they know damned fine there's no system to dispose of them is a mockery. The best solution I've heard so far is to drop them off a bridge over the Carlisle/Settle line when a coal train passes below. Some wag suggested if your timing was good enough you'd get it just in front of the train and have a claim as well.

You know - thingy!

I had a local farmer in my office, you know who I mean, matey from Wharton, farms at Moor End, can't just remember his name. We were carrying on like this and he asked me if I'd joined the CRAFT Society - CRAFT Society?

"Yes," he said - "Can't Remember a Flipping Thing." He was coming back with an application form as I'm getting all the right attributes - but he must have forgotten it!

Fat lambs

I was at the Easter Fat Show at Kirkby and was sure I was going to see my first £100 fat lamb. There were two Suffolk spring lambs at 45kg. that won the show. I still think they could be called baby lambs - poor little beggars haven't had much of a life. Anyway, the bidding started at such a rattle they were racing towards £100. My eyes about popped out of my head. They did get pulled up at £98.00 but they were still a fair go at that.

There's one or two old farmers bemoaning the fact they've no lambs left now the prices have improved. That's of course why the prices have improved.

IACS

I'M writing this at the end of April and the weather's just broken and I'm about mewed under with IACS forms. It's that wet week everyone's been waiting for to do their paperwork.

I am going to have a busy couple of weeks as folk seem to have been lambing later this year as well, so IACS has been a slow start and a chaotic finish. It's a bit like lambing at home when we loused all our tups at once. You knew the end of seventeen days would come and I know that the 15 May (closing date) will come. Phew.

A mystery

I spotted some walls covered with hessian sheeting and couldn't work out what was going on (see picture page 61). They were quite near a gentleman who keep horses so I thought he might be doing a bit of cross country and the bags were to save his horse's legs. Then I saw these bags appearing here, there and everywhere. The penny finally dropped, they were on the track of a new water-pipe that was being put in.

I am reliably informed the sheeting is to stop birds nesting in the walls so they don't disturb them when they come in with the diggers later in the year. Pity they didn't think as much about the farmers!

£12.50 hole

WE haven't had any lambing this time, but we've been to Uncle Bryan's a time or two. I was going to say to help, but I'm sure we'd be more of a hindrance than a help. We were in his old Daihatsu which was about out of diesel and running on fumes when Cousin Ian took it to Kirkby to fill it up, or so I thought. He'd hardly put anything in it so I said I'd have at least filled it up. "No," says Ian, "there's a hole at £12.50."

Can't knock Uncle Bryan and Cousin Ian though - three yows lambed - six lambs going- 200%.

Cool

AFTER my piece last month, I got interviewed on CFM about the bags on the wall. I told Can-R-Cum whose reply was: "CFM's cool Dad, they can't have you on." Oh dear, so I'm not cool any more, if I ever was.

Yow trade

THE sheep trade has been wonderful this spring with very few long faces in Kirkby on a Tuesday night. The yow price always slips after 15 May and someone was bemoaning the fact. After some thought, we still thought it was a lot better than the days of "Buy One Get a Penful Free."

CAP review 1

I was invited to a breakfast meeting of 25 professionals in Cumbria agriculture by HSBC Bank. In truth, it was 24 professionals and me. I asked if they were going to tell us about CAP Reform - the answer was a definite NO. They'd try and give advice once the decisions are made - very sensible. If you try to be one jump ahead of our European cousins you're probably jumping in the wrong direction.

CAP review 2

I heard a lovely one about an old farmer who was trying to take in all this new fangled jargon and was being told about de-coupling. He looked at his wife of many years and thought it was about time HE was decoupled too. And before you ask - no, it wasn't Uncle Bryan.

Grease lightening

IF you take the *Mail on Sunday* and got as far as the centre pages of the financial supplement you'd be able to read all about my colleague, Martin Jeal at Penrith putting in an eleven hour day. It made very good reading and showed the NFU Mutual in an excellent light. I wasn't sure if it was a work of fiction till I got to the bit where he described himself as coming out from under the duvet like "grease lightning" - doesn't bear thinking about.

PX03XWA

HE posed for a few pictures and one was very similar to the one here where I am trying a "Jeal-type" pose. I was very proud that unlike Martin I haven't got a personalised registration. My wife pointed out that I had - XWA stood for Xtra Wide A**e. I then had to explain to her very carefully that it wasn't her new car, it was mine.

I usually get quite a bit of stick when I get a fresh motor, but haven't really been bothered this time. I think I got more stick for running about in a four year old Ford Escort.

Fifteen - Love

I went on to a Limousin breeder's farm near Asby on a lovely sunny afternoon but couldn't find him and could only find his son. So I asked him where the old man was. "Oh, probably watching the tennis." I did think this was quite amusing but I have to add he actually wasn't watching the tennis but at Kirkby getting pipe fittings.

Can-R-Havacar

I'VE not written much about Can-R-Cum lately and if she's about you still struggle to go anywhere without her. At 16, she's getting to be a bit more of a "Can-R-Go" to Brough Club or as she approaches her 17th birthday - "Can-R-Havacar" - everybody else's dads bought them one.

Takes me back to when I was 17. I can remember after the first five minutes of my first driving lesson, the instructor saying to me: "You're a bloody farmer's son, aren't you." One hand on the steering wheel, crossing arms when cornering, etc, etc.

A Nice One

I heard this joke recently and it tickled me. A forgetful old man walks into a shop and looks awfully worried and tells the assistant he can't remember if he wants a camisole or a casserole. "Don't worry," says the assistant, "Is your bird dead or alive?"

Satisfaction

THE weather's just broken and I was asking someone if they'd got their crop. Yes, they had and there was no nicer noise than the sound of rain on plastic.

It's true, it was always a massive relief to finish hay, but it was always that much sweeter if it poured down the next day.

A Fair Mess

YOU'VE seen the romantic pictures of the old hooped caravans, you've watched the picturesque view of the black and white horses being washed in the River Eden, isn't it nostalgic and sentimental? Now, see the reality - a picture (on page 58) taken shortly after the travelling people have left Appleby.

I must admit you have to admire the organisers. You have got to be quick to get a picture like this as the clean up operation is fast and effective.

Dead or Alive

A farmer/haulier from Greenholme had had a bit of a heart do and as they say in the press 'reports of his death were greatly exaggerated' or as you and I would say, local gossip got out of hand. When he met one of his mates from a bit off he gave him a queer look and said: "Ah hope I look as good as you when ah'm deed!"

Walkers, Dogs and Cows

THE major topic at present when discussing insurance is footpaths and walkers with dogs. I think education is the answer, because I certainly wouldn't set my kids off through a field of cattle with a dog on a bit of string. I wouldn't be keen myself and I would know to kick the dog's backside if things got tricky. A lot of these walker-types think because they've got a right to exercise it comes hell or high water. As someone pointed out to me, you've every right to cross the road, but would you step out in front of a 35-ton artic?

History Lesson

WE have been doing a bit of spring cleaning in the office and came across a box of old minute books. I can tell you the first meeting at Appleby recorded was in 1930 when Tom Sisson was the secretary and J H Dent, the chairman.

Kirkby Stephen's inaugural meeting was 1929 and J Wood, the secretary, Michael Morland Sanderson of Heggerscales (my grandfather) was voted onto the committee and I can also tell you in 1941 he paid a subscription of 15/-. Records for Orton and Tebay branch also go back donkeys years and George Horn was branch chairman then as well!!

I see Jim Nicholson attended his first meeting in June 1966. If anyone would like to come in to have a look at them, they're more than welcome.

Father

MY father has always been a good source of amusing stories. He worked for his father-in-law, my grandfather and was always amused by his man management.

One farm worker was sent to bury the Suffolk tup which had passed away. It was a hot day, he was a big tup and it wasn't good digging. He was eventually buried, but his leg was sticking up between two of the sods. My grandfather wasn't much amused by this poor attempt but he said nothing. In fact he said nothing for ten days then he sent his men back to re-bury the tup. Ugh - just think what sort of a state it would be in. Everything was always buried deep enough after that.

My grandfather liked to keep his men working and always blacked my grandmother if the meals were too hot. "You'll skitter them lads with that hot porridge." It was really because they'd have to wait for it to cool. Father reckoned he was best after lunch. He'd jump up after his meal: "Well lads, come on, we'll have to get on," march out of the house and everyone would have to follow him. He'd do one lap of the yard and straight back in for his after-dinner nap.

Save and Spend

FATHER tells a lovely tale of an old farmer in the hills, never spent a penny and saved all his life. He was getting on and could make life much easier for himself and his wife - things like electric or a water closet, or even a holiday - but no the old lad wouldn't spend a penny. His friends and neighbours pointed out to him if he didn't spend it his son would and his son was of exactly the opposite persuasion. All the old lad would say was: "If he gets as much pleasure out of spending it as I've had of saving, then the job's alright."

Pay up?

ANOTHER nice one is the old lad who's been pestered by a particular rep (might even have been the NFU man). He's just about had enough and explains to the young man how he settles his outstanding bills. "At the end of each month, all the bills get put in a hat and I pull them out and pay them until the money runs out - and if you don't get off me back your bill won't even go in the bloody hat."

What a Summer

THE general consensus is it's been the best summer we've had for a lot of years with plenty of good weather for everyone to get their crop and harvest, a good dowsing of rain every now and again to keep everything growing. Wonderful. Nothing for farmers to complain about then - well - the only complaint I've heard is silage grass has been getting that dry it wouldn't blow into a trailer. It can't be bad if that's the only complaint. (Not forgetting lame sheep and wicks, of course).

What a Summer!

WITH such a good summer I'd have a wonderful week up the west coast of Scotland wouldn't I? Well, yes, if you like rain. I think we hit the only bad week in August. Still it was glorious at Nottingham and Leeds, so I could watch the cricket and you can still go seal spotting in the rain. It was that bad, we had rain water coming through the ceiling one morning and the next day the private water supply dried up. Gravel had washed into the header tank they claimed, and not a dead sheep as I suggested.

Poor Old Beggar

TUESDAY nights in Kirkby Auction are quite pleasant this back-end. Lambs are a decent trade and the crack's getting back to something like it used to be. They've put a fancy new screen in to show the weights and prices and I'm having to look very carefully to tell 3s and 8s apart. One or two more like me who aren't getting any younger are having the same problem.

There was great rejoicing in my family earlier this year. Son James (14) passed his big sister and his mother and is now the second tallest in the family. He waved his fist slowly at me and said: "I'll soon be as big as you dad."

I've just been completing my electoral role form and have had to put my daughter on it - Can-R-Vote! Poor old beggar!

Right to Roam Maps

THE second stage maps are out and anyone who put an appeal in should have been told if they've been successful or not. We seem to have been reasonably successful getting land taken out where it was obviously better grade land but not as successful with the more allotment type ground we weren't as hopeful about anyway. It's worth checking the new maps as there are odd pieces that weren't included and now are. Obviously the rambler/walker types have been having their input. I see Warcop Range is still designated as open country so no prizes for guessing where I think the ramblers should ramble.

The Full Monty

I'VE been coming in for some flack from some ex-county chairman for giving this year's incumbent an easy ride just coz he's my mate. Well, just to keep them happy, there's a picture of him organising the NFU Roadshow at Orton Farmers Market. Just a touch like Field Marshall Montgomery don't you think? See the photograph on page 62.

In my role with Appleby Show, I was attempting to get Mrs Cockbain to sign for the trophy she'd just won with her horse. She was too busy telling me Will had been recording a record - the mind boggles - is that Pop Idol or Bone Idle? - A cover version of the old Searchers *Needles and Pins* perhaps?

A Whitewash

IT'S been quiet in the NFU office while it's been hot and everyone's been silaging, haytiming, etc. so Tina's had a massive spring clean and thrown out numerous bags of papers. I took them to my mother-in-law's to burn and asked her if I could use father-outlaw's fire hole. Yes - as long as I finished her whitewashing. I told her I'd do that under consideration she didn't tell my wife. I didn't want Marian knowing I was capable of operating a paint brush. In the event, I got that much whitewash on myself it was obvious, and she wouldn't want me painting anything.

Hole in One

JUST imagine the picture. Uncle Bryan on his knees on the Kaber/Barras road looking as if he was praying for all our souls. The local farmer and quarryman from Borren House stops to see if he's taken one but Uncle's found a hole the size of a tin can in the road into a drain. Keith bends over to have a look and his mobile flies from his top pocket straight down the hole into the drain. It wasn't recovered until a council digger came some time later to make the road safe.

Uncle's still doing well on the lamb front. The kids have had two Beltex-X lambs away at 40kgs and £48 each.

Never Forget

WITH no farming, we get the odd day off and given their pick, the kids wanted to go to Knowsley Safari Park. It was quite good - you drove through a couple of hundred acres full of monkeys, buffaloes, ostriches, etc. The big cats were in large compounds and so were the elephants.

We were watching the elephants when one of the big ones deposited a large heap of elephant dung right in front of the crowd. It must have been three foot high. He then promptly turned round and started to pick it up with his trunk and eat it. This was pretty amusing but just as amusing was the reaction of all the townies round and about who were horrified. Our kids didn't think too much about it, as they said when you've seen an old yow bent like a U-bend eating her own cleansing this was a mere detail.

One Size Fits All

I'VE been getting a bit of stick in recent weeks as my wife has got a little job for the first time in 17 years. "Things must be bad at the NFU if you've got to send the wife out to work," etc. She was 'head-hunted' by Mr Pigney and is working in the shop. It has gone quite well but she was amused when David gave her the Pigney's pinny/tabard and he told her one size fits all. Don't think so David!!

On the Mat

I got a call that I had to go and see Mrs Heron at Warcop. I dutifully went as instructed and met her husband at the back door who informed me I was required for quarter of an hour on the carpet. Now I know an NFU man's duties are many and varied, but.... Anyway, I got in the house and the carpet was covered in maps. It was this digital mapping exercise and if anyone else out there would like a hand with their maps, you know where I am.

A Trip to Holland?

FATHER has been busy in his garden planting a few shrubs and such like. They weren't doing too well and couple developed yellow patches on them. He was puzzled and finally discovered his old dog was piddling on them. He was getting quite cross when we were there, as they were dear and was threatening to have Mr. Rap put down. Granda got reminded there were places in Holland you can send Grandas to get a similar job done. He had a rethink and went and rescued his old fire guards and put them in front of his shrubs.

Rudolf

ONE of my favourite foot and mouth stories is of the farmer down Penrith way who was determined not to get the disease and wouldn't let anyone from the Ministry on his farm. Eventually he had to give in but would only let the vet look at his stock out of his pick-up riding round the fields. He was taking this foreign vet around and the vet was determined he was going to get out among his cattle and the farmer was determined he wasn't. They were getting to falling out when the pick-up started to rock. "What's that?" asked the vet. "That's Rudolf and he ain't no reindeer." There was an enormous bull ratching his head on the back of the pick-up. The vet decided he didn't want to get out after all!

Big John Lancaster

WHEN this book was being put together all the contents of my 'writings file' were typed up for publication and included in it was what follows, which was the address I gave at John Lancaster's funeral. My first reaction was just leave it out, but after a bit of thought and consultation, I've left it in. I worked for John down at Kendal for ten very happy years in the 80s and he made a strong impact on my life and career. So here is my tribute to Big John:

It doesn't seem two minutes since I was stood in Whoop Hall poking fun at John at his retirement do. In fact it's two years gone November and he's been fighting cancer for all but five of those months - not the best of retirements.

I've worked alongside John for the NFU in some capacity for the last 27 years. I well know the respect he is held in by the farming community which is borne out by the number of people here today. What many may not be aware of is the esteem he is held in by his work colleagues. He did a wonderful job on our behalf when he was at the helm of our Group Secretaries Union. I was at a meeting when, completely unsolicited his praises were sung with regard to the deal he negotiated for our pensions, that's just a little ironic now.

I've always been aware of his strong love of his family - Cath, our Joanne, our Kirsty and our Richard, pick on them at your peril. His love of sport always came to the fore, no more than when he told you with great pride who our Richard had just steamrollered on the rugby field. He always encouraged me with my rugby, especially when we played

Kendal. John played rugby himself at Upper Wharfedale where Richard has followed in his footsteps.

Richard tells me he will be missed there especially by the referees who will struggle to manage without the loud verbal advice from the touchline. He also played cricket at Sedgwick which was a family affair, playing alongside Richard with Cath catering and the girls scoring. He was also a fisherman and took up golf in later life.

My favourite memory of my time working for John was in the summer of 1981. On a Tuesday morning we went over how Ian Botham had clattered the Aussies for 149no. John went home for his dinner and rang the office right away: "You'd better come and watch this," he said. We both witnessed probably the greatest upset in test cricket in our dinner hour.

John never did things by half. His appeal for the orphanage in Rumania with his daughter Kirsty was a marvellous example of that as indeed was all his work for the farming community. I know one of his proudest moments was receiving his honourary membership of Sedbergh Branch. The plaque is on his sitting room wall and I don't know of any other NFU Group Secretary with such an honour.

Big John was always larger than life. Right up front with you, a spade was a spade. Nothing was said that didn't need saying and nothing was missed that did need saying; everything was out in the open

The farming community and the local community for which he did much work owe him a debt of gratitude as do all my colleagues and not least of all myself. Here I am doing something I've never done before - he's still influencing me. Big John - a big man - in every sense of the word.

MORE BOOKS FROM HAYLOFT

Yows & Cows, A Bit of Westmorland Wit, Mike Sanderson
(£7.95, ISBN 0 9523282 0 8)

To Bid Them Farewell, A Foot & Mouth Diary, Adam Day
(£14.50, ISBN 190 452 4109)

The Herdwick Country Cook Book, Hugh & Therese Southgate
(Hardback, £29.95, ISBN 0954071182/ Paperback, £14.95, ISBN 0954071174)

Those Were the Days, An Entertainment Revue of Carlisle, 1950-70, Marie
K Dickens & Geoff Dickens (£22.90, ISBN 190 452 4125)

Oil, Sand & Politics, Dr. Philip Horniblow (£25, ISBN 190 452 4095)

*Running High, The First Continuous Traverse of the 303 Mountains of
Britain and Ireland,* Hugh Symonds, (£16.99, ISBN 190 452 415X)

From the High Pennines, A History of the Alderson Family,
Marmaduke Alderson, (£10.00, ISBN 190 452 4079)

The Maddison Line, A Journalist's Journey around Britain, Roy Maddison
(£10.00, ISBN 1 9045240 6 0)

Pashler's Lane, A Clare Childhood, Elizabeth Holdgate
(£10.00, ISBN 095 4207203)

The Long Day Done, Jeremy Rowan-Robinson
(£9.50, ISBN 1 9045240 4 4)

Odd Corners in Appleby, Gareth Hayes (£8.50, ISBN 1 9045240 0 1)

The Ghastlies, Trix Jones and Shane Surgey (£3.99, ISBN 1 9045240 4 4)

A Journey of Soles, Lands End to John O'Groats, Kathy Trimmer
(£9.50, 1 9045240 5 2)

*Changing the Face of Carlisle, The Life and Times of Percy Dalton, City
Engineer and Surveyor, 1926-1949,* Marie K. Dickens
(£8, ISBN 0 9540711 9 0)

*From Clogs and Wellies to Shiny Shoes, A Windermere Lad's Memories
of South Lakeland,* Miles R. M. Bolton (£12.50, ISBN 1 9045240 2 8)

A History of Kaber, Helen McDonald and Christine Dowson,
(£8, ISBN 0 9540711 6 6)

The Gifkin Gofkins, Irene Brenan (£2.50, ISBN 1 9045240 1 X)

*A Dream Come True, the Life and Times of a Lake District National
Park Ranger,* David Birkett (£5.50, ISBN 0 9540711 5 8)

Gone to Blazes, Life as a Cumbrian Fireman, David Stubbings
(£9.95, ISBN 0 9540711 4 X)

Changing Times, A History of Bolton, Barbara Cotton
(£12.50, ISBN 0 9540711 3 1)

Better by Far a Cumberland Hussar, A History of the Westmorland and Cumberland Yeomanry, Colin Bardgett
(Hardback, £26.95, ISBN 0954071123/ Paperback, £16.95, ISBN 0954071115)

Northern Warrior, the Story of Sir Andreas de Harcla, Adrian Rogan
(£8.95, ISBN 0 9523282 8 3)

A Riot of Thorn & Leaf, Dulcie Matthews (£7.95, ISBN 0 9540711 0 7)

Military Mountaineering, A History of Services Expeditions, 1945-2000
Retd. SAS Major Bronco Lane
(Hardback, £25.95, ISBN 0952328216/Paperback, £17.95, ISBN 0952328267)

2041 - The Voyage South, Robert Swan (£8.95, 0 9523282 7 5)

Riding the Stang, Dawn Robertson (£9.99, ISBN 0 9523282 2 4)

Secrets and Legends of Old Westmorland, Peter Koronka & Dawn Robertson
(Hardback, £17.95, ISBN 0 9523282 4 0)
(Paperback, £11.95, ISBN 0 9523282 9 1)

The Irish Influence, Migrant Workers in Northern England,
Harold Slight (£4.95, 0 9523282 5 9)

Soldiers and Sherpas, A Taste for Adventure, Brummie Stokes.
(£19.95, 0 9541551 0 6)

North Country Tapestry, Sylvia Mary McCosh (£10, 0 9518690 0 0)

Between Two Gardens, The Diary of two Border Gardens,
Sylvia Mary McCosh (£5.95, 0 9008111 7 X)

Dacre Castle, A short history of the Castle and the Dacre Family,
E. H. A. Stretton (£5.50, 0 9518690 1 9)

Little Ireland, Memories of a Cleator Moor Childhood, Sean Close
(£7.95, ISBN 095 4067 304)

A Slip from Grace, More tales from Little Ireland, Sean Close
(£10.00, ISBN 095 4067 312)

You can order any of our books by writing to:
Hayloft Publishing Ltd., South Stainmore, Kirkby Stephen,
Cumbria, CA17 4EU, UK.
Please enclose a cheque plus £2 for UK postage and packing.
or telephone: +44 (0)17683) 42300
For more information see: www.hayloft.org.uk